Living The Blessed Life

Unless otherwise indicated, Bible quotations are taken from the New American Standard Version of the Bible.

Published in Nashville, Tennessee by Berean Publishing House
Copyright © 2012 Clinton M. Lewis, Sr.

ISBN: 0-6156-9342-3
ISBN-13: 9780615693422

Living The Blessed Life

What Does It Really Mean To Be Blessed By God?

Clinton M. Lewis, Sr.
Foreword by: Pastor James "Tex" Thomas

Table Of Contents

FOREWORD

In the last ten years, the Church has been through some theological storms. Of the many rocks that have come to land have been questions about prosperity, how God blesses and why.

It has been said, inherent in the idea of blessing is the invocation of special favor on a person or object that is held in high esteem. The objects of blessing in the Old Testament maybe either divine or human, or that which belongs to either God or human beings.

When God is the object of human blessing, the context is invariably one of worship and praise. When people bless God, they offer him praise for who he is and what he has done on behalf of those he love.

It is said that the most well-known "blessings" are described in the Beatitudes, wherein we see the various kinds of blessings God gives to those who are worthy of these graces. I am so grateful that we have a young profound and able, Pastor Clinton M. Lewis, Sr., to give our congregations some light on this subject.

Pastor James "Tex" Thomas
Jefferson Street Baptist Church
Nashville, TN

ACKNOWLEDGEMENTS

I thank God for this privilege of being able to further a great work He called me to do in proclaiming His holy word. This is another venue I have been afforded with to share His good news. It has not been an easy journey, there have been pitfalls and roadblocks along the way. But, right now I pause to praise God for keeping this vision ever before me.

I want to thank my wife, Kia, for her persistent prayers for me and the ministry I am called to perform, for her willingness to pour into me and encourage me in all that I attempt to do for God's glory. I thank you, Kia, for taking up my slack! I want to thank my children, Devon, Clinton, Jr., Maurie, Jon and Jordan, for their understanding of my role as a pastor over these seventeen years. Many times, the demands of being a pastor has caused them to sacrifice much needed time with me.

And lastly, I want to thank the Mount Hopewell Baptist Church, and our wonderful staff. What a joy it is to serve such a wonderful as you! Specifically, I do want to acknowledge and thank Andre Trice for your passionate support to the administrative demands I have as a pastor, and in my extended areas of ministries.

In closing, I want to acknowledge and dedicate this book in the memory of the "Paul" in my life, Pastor Curtis Walter Goodwin, Sr. I will forever be indebted to his labor of love and example of pastoral ministry in my life. Love you forever and always "Rev."

INTRODUCTION

There is much confusion within the interpretation and application of Judean-Christian Scripture (specifically referring to the Old and New Testament writings of the Holy Bible) concerning our understanding of the blessings of God in our individual lives. Although it has never faded or ceased to be in existence since the first century Christians; during the past few years, there seems to be a greater or renewed emphasis being placed on prosperity ministries and theology. In essence, prosperity theology is the teaching that an authentic religious belief and behavior in a person will result in their material prosperity, affluence, or richness. That is, this teaching holds that material prosperity, particularly financial prosperity and success in business and personal life, is to be expected as external evidence of God's favor.

Is this the totality of God's teaching on His blessings, His favor, or prosperity for believers? Is an individual's health or wealth directly correlated with one's level of spirituality? Many people of faith so frequently use such expressions as, "I am blessed and highly favored. I am blessed of the Lord." But, what does it really mean to be blessed by God? What is the actual Biblical teaching and practical understanding an individual believer can hold on to as it relates to God's blessings for his or her life?

In order to properly answer these questions and to fully enjoy living a "blessed life" of, from and through our God, this book will highlight the more proper balance that an individual's "prosperity" is more spiritual than physical (including wealth and health emphasis). As we prepare to revisit this journey of re-ordering our priorities (meaning spiritual blessings supersede material/physical blessings), we will do so by journeying through themes from the Sermon on the Mount, as given by Jesus in the fifth chapter of the Gospel of Matthew.

When you carefully study the Bible, you will see that from the first verse in chapter one of the book of Genesis to the twenty-first verse of the twenty-second chapter of the book of Revelations, the Word of God has constantly declared His people as "blessed", "being blessed", or God is viewed as conferring or giving "blessings" to humanity. After God had created both Adam and Eve—Adam from the dust of the earth and Eve from the side of the first human, Adam—Genesis 1:28 states that God then *blessed* then and said, "Be fruitful and multiply, and fill the earth, and subdue it; and rule over the fish of the sea and over the birds of the sky and over every living thing that moves on the earth." The Apostle John, while in exile on the Island of Patmos, was allowed by God to share in a vision of the realities of the end of times. In the prophetic book of Revelations, in particular Rev. 22:12-14, John records Jesus as saying, "Behold, I am coming quickly and My reward is with Me, to render to every man according to what he has done. I am the Alpha and the Omega, the first and the last, the beginning and the end. Blessed are those who wash their robes, so that they may have the right to the tree of life, and may enter by the gate into the city."

Throughout its pages, the Word of God is filled with God's pronouncements of blessings. In Psalms 1:1, David says, "How blessed is the man who does not walk in the counsel of the wicked, nor stand in the path of sinners, nor sit in the seat of scoffers." The eighty-fourth Psalms records the psalmist writing, "How blessed is the man whose strength is in You, whose heart are the highways to Zion!" (Psalms 84:5). In Acts 20:35, the Apostle Paul quotes the words of Jesus by saying, "It is more blessed to give than to receive." And even in our focal passage of Scripture for the thesis of this book (the fifth chapter of Matthew), Jesus looks at the multitude that had gathered around Him on that particular day, He ascends further up the mountain with His twelve disciples and says to the twelve and the multitudes, "Blessed are the poor in spirit....Blessed are they that mourn...Blessed are the meek...Blessed are they which do hunger and thirst after righteousness....Blessed are the merciful...Blessed are the pure in heart... Blessed are the peacemakers...Blessed are they which are persecuted for righteousness sake...Blessed are you when people insult you and persecute you, and falsify all kinds of evil against you because of Me."

These passages, among others, demonstrate that God has consistently declared His blessings upon His people. However, the way many people interpret, teach, preach and apply these declarations from Scripture is a great indication that many fully don't understand what it means to be blessed by God. In this growing movement of spirituality in our land, it is evident that to be blessed by God is what many people are seeking. It is obvious that to be blessed by God is what many people want or desire. However, the contention is made that the problem is that many people are seeking the blessings of God from or in the *things* of this world. Many people of faith are guilty of limiting the blessings of God to positions, money, fame, fortunes, earthly power, and sensual or temporal pleasure.

Let me clearly state, that I am a firm believer that God blesses us in various forms and ways. God blesses us in physical and tangible ways. But, the blessings of God begin before and far surpasses any physical blessing we could ever receive from God. God blesses us monetarily—but money will still act funny. God blesses us with homes—but homes can still be foreclosed. God blesses us with cars—but cars can still be repossessed. God blesses us with healings for our bodies—but our bodies will still deteriorate and fade away into a physical death. As evidenced by the words of Jesus in the 6th chapter of Matthew, the chapter which immediately follows the Beatitudes or the nine statements of blessings, Jesus said, "Do Not store up for yourselves the treasures on earth, where moth and rust destroy, and where thieves break in and steal. But store up for yourselves treasures in heaven, where neither moth nor rust destroys, and where thieves do not break in or steal; for where your treasure is, there your heart will be also." (Matthew 6:19-21).

In order to begin this journey of answering the question raised in the title of this book, you first must have a clear understanding of the difference between being blessed and being happy. There are some versions of the Bible which translate the word "blessed" as happy. However, when you conduct a serious word study of the word "blessed", you will discover that the word "happy" does not do it enough justice. The word "blessed" literally means a spiritual joy and a spiritual satisfaction which lasts regardless of outward conditions or surroundings. This deeper understanding of the word "blessed" means that our spiritual joy will carry us through praise and pain, through singing and sorrow, through glory and grief, through laughter and loss. Being called the blessed of God means that you have a joy which is serene and untouchable. It means that you a joy that is completely independent of all of the chances or changes of this life.

However, the word "happiness" stands in total contrast to the word "blessed." It is not a good translation for the word blessed. In the word "happiness" the root word, hap, literally means chance. Therefore, human happiness is dependent and contingent upon the positive agents in the changes of life. Human happiness is a status or virtue that the circumstances of life can give, and it's the status or virtue that the circumstances of life can take away. Happiness is conditional. Happiness is dependent on your surroundings. But, the blessedness of and from God goes beyond being happy—the blessedness of God is completely untouchable by the events of life. Jesus states, "No one will take your joy from you" (John 16:22).

In addition to clearing up the differences between blessed and happy or happiness, if we are going to properly answer the book's title question, we have to also realize that being blessed means we have a spiritual joy with is eternal. The word eternal is best described as enduring or everlasting. Therefore, since we are the blessed of God, we have a spiritual joy that will see us through our pains, sorrows, losses and our grief. It is eternal. Even the negative events that we all must face and encounter in this life are powerless against our joy. Yes, you may weep because the pain will hurt. You may even cry because the sorrows of life will wound or impair you. However, as children of God, never should we weep or cry as those who have no hope. David, one of the psalmists, reminds us that weeping may endure for only one night, but joy will come in the morning (Psalm 30:5).

We are the blessed people of God. God has given us the spiritual fruit of joy to carry us through every pain and moment of grief. The blessed of God have a joy that is unspeakable, and a joy that is eternal. There is a beautiful story that highlights the testimony of a man by the name of Robert Reed which is demonstrative of the truths of both an unspeakable and eternal joy. Whenever Robert would share his testimony, he would always graciously state that he had everything he needed to maintain his spirit of joy. However, the living, visible picture of Robert is that his hands are twisted—his feet are useless—he can't feed or bathe himself—he can't brush his teeth or comb his hair—his speech is slurred—and his shirts are held together by Velcro. Robert has cerebral palsy, but he has everything he needs for joy. His illness did not keep him from graduating from college or from teaching at a junior college in St. Louis. Neither did his disease prevent him from serving as a missionary in Portugal. One day Robert was preparing to share his testimony with others and some men had to carry him in his wheelchair onto the raised platform. Those same men had to lay his Bible in his lap. Robert then took his stiff fingers to turn the pages of the Bible. While he was turning the pages, the people in the audience began to wipe away the tears falling from their eyes as they watched him with admiration. Robert did not ask for their pity or sympathy. Robert, however, did the very opposite. He held his bent hand up in the air and cried out in a voice of praise, "I have everything I need for joy!" His shits are held together by Velcro strips, but his life is held together by joy. Likewise, things in your life may never be the way you desire for them to be, but thank God that His joy is holding you together.

Chapter 1
Blessed Are The Poor In Spirit

Some time ago I saw this poster which included the following message: "A Prayer to be said, when the world has gotten you down, and you feel rotten, and you are too doggone tired to pray, and you are in a big hurry, and besides, you are mad at everybody........HELP!"

The majority of people, especially in this western culture, have been taught to be independent, indispensable, stubborn and supper efficient. For many people, there is an inner voice or drive that says, "Prove it to them! You can do it! You don't need anyone's help! You can do it all by yourself!" At the very heart of our problem is pride. And for some it is the single greatest obstacle or detriment in keeping them from coming into a saving relationship through Jesus Christ. In addition, this personal problem of pride is hindering the spiritual growth and maturity of some professed believers.

King Saul of Israel is a prime example of this particular spiritual problem of pride. Saul was approximately forty years old when he began to reign as king over Israel. He had a problem with pride that he never dealt with, and this problem became his downfall. In the biblical story of Saul, his son, Jonathan, smote or struck down the garrison of the Philistines in Geba, and his father stole the show. I Samuel 13:3-4 states, "Jonathan smote the garrison of the Philistines that was in Geba, and the Philistines heard of it. Then Saul blew the trumpet throughout the land, saying, "Let the Hebrews hear." All Israel heard the news that Saul had smitten the garrison of the Philistines, and also that Israel had become odious to the Philistines. The people were then summoned to Saul at Gilgal." This story reveals that Saul received the credit at the expense of someone else's work because of his own disposition of cheap pride and vainglory. This story is just one of many examples of the wicked pride of Saul. The historical presentation of Saul is that he was disobedient to the core—so much to the point that the word of the Lord came to the prophet Samuel saying, "I regret that I have made Saul king, for he has turned his back from following me and has not carried out my commandments. And Samuel was distressed and cried out to the Lord all night. Samuel rose early in the morning to meet Saul; and it was told Samuel saying, "Saul came to Carmel, and behold he set up a monument for himself, then turned and proceeded on down to Gilgal." Samuel came to Saul, and Saul said to him, "Blessed are you of the Lord." But Samuel said, "What then is this bleating of the sheep in my ears, and the lowing of the oxen which I hear?" Saul said, "They have brought them from the Amalekites, for the people spared the best of the sheep and oxen to sacrifice to the Lord your God; but the rest we have utterly destroyed."" (I Samuel 15:10-15). Saul stooped so low as to try to use worship as a scheme to cover his trickery. Finally, God rejected Saul as king, because Saul had rejected the word of God (I Samuel 15:23-26).

The principal which is found in this observation of Saul's life is pride. As a matter of fact, the writings of I Samuel 16:7 states it quite clearly, "The Lord said to Samuel, "Do not look at his appearance or at the height of his stature, because I have rejected him; for God sees not as man sees, for man looks at the outward, but the Lord looks at the heart."" King Saul had a problem with pride and he did not want to face his problem. Just as Saul was blinded by the sin of pride in his life, so many of us today are just as blinded and guilty as well.

In the seventh chapter of the gospel according to Matthew, Jesus gives a prophetic picture of the final day. In essence and in paraphrase, Jesus said, "Many will say to me on that day, Lord, Lord, did we not prophesy in your name, and in your name drive out demons and perform many miracles?" Surprisingly, this picture as presented in Matthew's writing is that of a vast of people standing before the throne of god bragging about themselves and their works. The great trumpet has sounded, and they are still tooting their own horns. Rather than singing the praises of God, they are steadily singing their own praises. Rather than worshipping God, they are reciting the deeds of their resumes. When they should be speechless, they speak. In the very presence of the King of kings, there will be a group that will boast of themselves. But, as this prophetic picture continues to unfold, Jesus then said, "I will say to them on that day, depart from me, I never knew you!"

When you look at the prophetic picture of the Last Day, it reminds us that being with God on heaven is not based on what we do on earth. It is not based on how well we perform in our services in this life. It is not based on our outward performances, nor is it based on our doing the right things. Being with God in heaven is based on something more profound—yet more simple. Our presence with God in heaven is based on something more meaningful that the right actions or the right activities we perform in this life. After all, you can do all of the right things with the wrong motive, spirit and heart.

There has got to be more to it than that.

Jesus said you are blessed when you realize that you are poor in spirit. In other words, you are blessed when you realize that you are living life in spiritual poverty. Being poor in spirit does is not in any way referring that a person must be poverty stricken and financially poor. I don't believe that people consistently and repetitively living in a state of hunger, nakedness and in slums are pleasing to God, especially when considering how plentiful the resources in this world. Even though Jesus said we would have the poor always with us, He also expects His followers and believers to do our part in elevating the poor. As it relates to this topic on the Sermon on the Mount, Jesus is not referring to those in material poverty. Rather, He means exactly what He says, "Blessed are the poor in spirit."

Being poor in spirit means you have acknowledged your spiritual helplessness and need before God. It means you have acknowledged the fact that you will face this life and life eternal apart from God. Being poor in spirit means you have realized that the most pure and precious blessings in this life comes by having a right relationship with God.

A good illustration of what it means to be poor in spirit is to just take a look at the very opposite meaning of this phrase—and that is having a spirit which is full of self. And for many people it is this spirit of selfishness, self-centeredness, and egotism that has and will keep them from having a relationship with God through the acceptance of His gift, grace and mercy through Jesus. Many people with this view of their own lives, this view of self-centeredness, falsely believe they can keep themselves better than God can. Some even think they can save themselves. But if you want to really be blessed, and I am not talking about being blessed by temporal things, but if you want to receive the blessings of God which is an unspeakable, bountiful joy which surpasses every hill and every valley, every smile and every tear, every up and every down that you can and will experience in this life there are a few things you have to remember.

Recognize the Problem

One thing I have discovered in my time of sharing with individuals who are recovering from alcohol and substance abuse, many recovering addicts have informed me that they could never deal with their problems with drug or alcohol until they were ready to recognize that a problem existed. Many have even stated that past attempts at recovery failed because of their reluctance to recognize their problem.

Don't fool yourselves—we are all addicts. Thank God that some of us are recovering addicts, but we were all addicts. Every person born in this world has a physical addiction to something in this world, it could have been an addiction to tell lies, an addiction to have premarital sex or post-marital sex with someone other than your spouse, an addiction to steal, to sell or use drugs, to spread rumors, to gossip, or an addiction to dishonor your parents. Everybody's addiction is different from the other person's, but everyone is an addict or either an "ex-something."

You can never deal with a problem until you recognize that the problem exists. Jesus told the story of a Jewish man who had two sons. The younger son asked for his share of his father's estate and journeyed into a distant Gentile country. The younger son squandered his money with wild, reckless living. He wasted the whole sum with the wildest unrestrained extravagance. Things went great until he ran out of money. As you continue to read this story from the fifteenth chapter of the Gospel according to Luke, you will discover that as soon as he spent everything he had, a severe famine occurred in that country and he began to be impoverished. He joined himself or became employed by a hog farmer—and the farmer sent the young man into the fields to feed his hogs. This young man found himself living life out of place—working with hogs, sleeping with hogs, and eating with hogs. But—when he came to his senses, he said, "How many of my father's hired men have more than enough bread, but I am dying here with hunger. I will get up and go to my father, and will say to him, "Father, I have sinned against heaven and in your sight; I am no longer worthy to be called your son; make me as one of your hired men.""

In contrast to King Saul, this young man came to his senses—literally. He came under great conviction in a moment of self-realization. He had been "beside" himself. But, he came to a deep realization of his spiritual need and he repented—he had a change of mind and heart. Look carefully at the symbolism.......the young man realized that all of the servants of his father had more than enough bread to eat, but he (the son) was starving in the hog pen. His father's servants had an abundance, but he was starving. Just like this young man, all of us must come to the point where we realize that all the riches of heaven are at our disposal—but we chose to sit, sulk, and complain in a pigsty. All the power of God rests upon us when we claim our inheritance. And once we claim our inheritance, we live as heirs of God and draw from God's riches.

We are sons and daughters of God—and not a slave.

But, the only way you can get out of a pigsty is to come to your senses and confess, "I have a problem." This problem that many people have: you can't think your way out of it, you can't spend your way out of it, you can't work your way out of it. You can't drink or drug your way out of this problem. The only way out of this problem is Jesus. Jesus did say, "I am the way, the truth and the light."

Blessed are the poor in spirit. The word used for "poor" describes a state of absolute poverty. In the Greek language, the root word means to crouch or to cower. This word describes the state of poverty that will beat you to the knees. In a physical sense, it gives us portrait of a beggar who has nothing at all and must live on other men's labors. He is so poor that he only obtains his daily living by begging. Not only has he been reduced to the very act of begging, but he covers his face with his hands in an act of being ashamed to let the giver know his true identity. He is living a life in absolute destitution.

That is the portrait and description of the word poor in the physical sense. But to be poor in spirit means that one has become conscious of his or her spiritual destitution. It is a painful experience to see yourself for who you really are. But the good news is that the spiritually poor person is aware of his condition and has enough pain to seek relief.

Isaiah 6:5 reminds us of such a response. In the year that King Uzziah died, Isaiah saw the Lord high and lifted up. Isaiah saw the glory of God for the very first time. He saw the angels worshipping and praising God. He saw the seraphim and cherubim praising God. And then the fifth verse of chapter six records Isaiah as saying in response to this atmosphere of holiness, "Woe is me, for I am a man of unclean lips." The prophet Isaiah came to grips with his own spiritual needs. He gives these words as an expression of his pain.

That is the journey we all must take. The Holy Spirit brings us to the place where we realize that we are not as spiritually prosperous and mature as we thought we were. But, our journey ends—yet begins when we cry out, "I am a sinner. I have a need. I have a problem. God, I want your help!" But, if you never come to that point, you will never get any help!

Help! Help! Help! I need help!

The old hymnologist of the church, Annie S. Hawkins, cried out, "I need thee every hour most gracious Lord. No tender voice like thine can peace afford. I need thee every hour, stay thou nearby. Temptations lose their power when thou art nigh. I need thee every hour, in joy or pain. Come quickly and abide, or life is in vain. I need thee, O, I need thee, Every hour—I need thee. O bless me now my Savior, I come to thee." (Hawkins, #229). This hymn echoes the theme that the first step to spiritual joy and riches is to realize just how poor you are. In order to taste of God's presence, you have to declare spiritual bankruptcy. In order to taste of God's presence, you have to acknowledge that you are in a spiritual crisis—you have to acknowledge that your cupboard is empty—you have to acknowledge that you pockets are empty—you have to know that all of your options are gone, but God Himself!

To experience the blessed joy of God, you can't brag—but you have to beg.

Receive the Promise

After you have realized that you have a problem, then and only then can you receive the promise. Jesus said, "Blessed are the poor in spirit, for theirs is the kingdom of heaven." (Matthew 5:3).

You should realize that two steps are taken by the person who realizes that he or she is spiritually poor. First, he turns his attention from the things of this world. The reason this step occurs is because he has come to the realization that nothing or no person in this world can make him spiritually rich. Secondly, she turns her attention strictly to God and His kingdom.

Thank God that His Word teaches that we all can experience a coming out party.

Come out of your poverty, it is the only way you can become more like Jesus. You can not stay the way you are and become like Him. You must experience a change in your nature. Come out of your poverty, it is the only way you can become a better witness. Come out of your poverty, it is the only way you can become all that Christ wants you to be. Come out of your poverty, it is the only way you can become a person who can walk in the fullness of God's blessings.

The question was once asked, "What is the kingdom of heaven like?" This question was asked of Jesus to mankind, and then he began to answer his own question by saying, "the kingdom of heaven is like a grain of mustard seed which a man took and sowed in his field—the least of all seeds, but when it is grown it is the greatest of all herbs. It is liken unto leaven, which a woman took and hid in three measures of meal, till the whole was leavened. It is liken unto a treasure hid in a field, the which when a man has found, he hides, and for the joy thereof he goes and sells all that he has and buys the field. The kingdom of heaven is liken unto a merchant man, seeking goodly pearls, who when he found one pearl of great price, went and sold all that he had and bought it." When Jesus spoke of the kingdom of heaven he spoke of those who found it and experienced great joy.

In other words, when a person discovers and discerns just how poor, broke, destitute, disgusted, frustrated, unfulfilled, unsatisfied, empty and void he is—then and only then can he experience true joy.

So, what is the kingdom of heaven? It is having joy in the midst of sorrow. It is having hope for tomorrow. It is having a bridge over troubled waters. It is having strength in the face of weakness. It is having a sure staff for your every leaning moment. It is having peace in the midst of confusion. It is having Jesus as your heart fixer and mind regulator.

When Jesus spoke of experiencing the kingdom of heaven—it was never exclusively in terms of a distant place or time, but rather when Jesus spoke of the kingdom of heaven, he spoke in terms of our experiencing a foretaste of heaven in the here and now. We can experience heaven while living on earth. However, while enjoying a foretaste of heaven now—we do hold fast to the promised reality that is yet to come that the best is yet to come!

There is a story of a lady who was considered to be a woman of status and class. A very humble woman, yet she appreciated the finer things of life. As time marched on, she found herself battling a terminal illness. After some time when it was discovered that healing was not coming her way, she boldly accepted God's way of ultimate healing—and that is for the believer experiencing victory through death. Upon the acceptance of the reality of her death, she asked for her pastor to come to her bedside so together they may plan her funeral. Her pastor came, and while attending her bedside they planned which scriptures were to be read, they planned the music for her celebration of life, together they selected those who would share in prayers and words of hope and comfort. After they finalized the funeral arrangements, the woman shared with her pastor that she had one more request of him. She said, "Pastor, make sure they bury me with a fork in my hand." Her pastor had a puzzling look on his face. But she said, "I know you are puzzled as to why I want to be buried with a fork in my hand. But pastor you know that I loved attending the fine banquets. And the one thing that always stood out to me is after I finished each course—the server would always say to me, "Keep your fork, the best is yet to come." Pastor, it did not matter if it was three course or a four course meal—at the last was my favorite part of the meal—it was desert time. And, pastor that is what I want people to know about me when they see me in my casket with a fork in my hand—just tell them that the best is yet to come!"

Blessed are the poor in spirit, for theirs is the kingdom of heaven—the best is yet to come!

Chapter 2
Blessed Are They That Mourn

As we continue to look at this sermon of Jesus, that we affectionately call the Sermon on the Mount, Jesus begins this sermon with the word "blessed" and continued to use this word for a total of nine times throughout the duration of this sermon on the mountainside.

Throughout our virtuous, vigorous voyage of this mystical and often times misunderstood momentous discussion of being blessed by God, it has been determined that being blessed by God goes beyond happiness. It has been established that the word "blessed" is better translated as having a spiritual joy and satisfaction that lasts regardless of your condition.

However, in this portion of the Sermon on the Mount, there is a paradoxical statement that is being presented by Jesus. There is a position that is expressed by our Lord and Savior which seems to be self-contradicting or absurd, but in reality expresses a truth. The paradoxical position in this sermon as Jesus looks upon this crowd is—if they mourn, how can they be blessed? Reality takes the position in all of our lives that there is no joy in mourning time! That is reality. But faith declares that we all can experience a spiritual joy that lasts and far exceeds our mournful situations.

We are called to grow and mature in our faith to the point that we can become living paradoxes. Living a life where we display joy unspeakable, while dwelling among so much sadness. Living a life where we are always at a spiritual high, but living at the lowest rung of life's ladder.

Blessed are they that mourn....

When you carefully look at the Bible, it speaks of at least three distinct types or forms of mourning. Usually when we hear of the word "mourning", we are most likely thinking of someone grieving over a tumultuous illness or dealing with the freshness of the recent bereavement of a loved one or a dear friend. For example, when David's son was born and illness touched his young, tender body so much to the point that the young child was lying at death's door, David tore his clothes, he fasted and prayed and laid on the ground of the floor of his son's room. David mourned. Also, when we hear the word "mourning" you can think of one having a feeling of pain as he looks at and realizes the sinfulness of the state of the world. Such is the case with Jesus as He wept over the sinfulness of the city of Jerusalem in Matthew 23:37-38 where He cried out, "O Jerusalem, Jerusalem, you who kill the prophets and stone those sent to you, how often I have longed to gather your children together as a hen gathers her chicks under her wings, but you were not willing. Look, your house is left to desolate." We, too, should have such a deep compassion as to weep over the injustice, the cruelty, the immorality and the lack of integrity that exists in our society today. The stated points are usually the positions we take when think of the word "mourning", but in the context of Matthew 5:4, the word "mourning" goes beyond these positions.

Many times we are guilty of wanting to quote this text and us it as consolation when we have just left hospital and the doctors have given up on our loved one. Many are guilty of only wanting to quote this text when they have just left the grave yard bidding their last farewell to a fallen saint. "Blessed are they that mourn, for they shall be comforted" sounds real good to our ears during our personal times of sorrow and grief. But strictly quoting this text at funerals or other sad situations is to use it out of its context or biblical perspective. We need to remember that God has provided for us other passages of scripture which are more appropriate to comfort us in our times of sorrow and grief. David gives us two such passages as, "Weeping may endure for a night, but joy comes in the morning," and from pains of what appeared to be almost certain death he said, "Yea, though I walk through the valleys of the shadow of death, I will fear no evil for you are with me. Your rod and staff comfort me." John while exile on the Isle of Patmos encourages us through such words as, "And God shall wipe away every tear from their eyes..." Yes, there is so much comfort found in God's word to aide us in our times of sorrow and grief. But, on the Sermon on the Mount, Jesus promises us comfort for a different type of mourning experience.

The Greek word used for "mourning" (pentheo) in this text and verse is the same Greek word used for mourning as it relates to grieving over the experience of a physical death. The word pentheo (pen-theh-o) literally means to grieve or to wail—it means to have a broken heart. This is the strongest word possible for mourning. It is sorrow—a desperate helpless type of sorrow. That is the portrait of the word "mourning" in Matthew 5:4. So, the question becomes—if Jesus is not talking about mourning because of or over physical death, what it is He equating this death-like grieving experience with? And the answer is that a self-realization of our own personal sins—a brokenness of self that comes from seeing Christ on the cross, yet realizing that it was our sins that put Him there will make you mourn, moan and groan.

I want to suggest that the eight beatitudes are arranged in four pairs, with the first pair being: Blessed are the poor in spirit, for theirs is the kingdom of heaven and Blessed are they that mourn, for they shall be comforted. This pair suggests that after you come to the self-realization of just how spiritually empty, poor, bankrupt and devastated you are—this reality check or understanding of yourself will make you cry.

When You See Yourself As Jesus Sees You—You Will Mourn

The sad reality is that some people never experience or realize the promised comfort of Jesus—they never realize the soul soothing and soul satisfaction that God has already provided through His Son, Jesus Christ, because they never accept or see who they really are. The truth of the matter is that many of us are guilty of having a "short-term or selective memory." We selectively forget about our faults and failures, our mistakes and mishaps, our issues and our secret illnesses. We bury these situations in what appears to be a hidden part of our mind. Many people never deal with some real issues that are present in their lives. But, when you truly deal with these secret, hidden, and seeming buried issues and truly see yourself for the very first time—it will make you weep, it will make you mourn and cry, it will make you wail and lament. But, I want you to know that is not a bad position to be—for then you are on the road of being healed through your tears.

The first verse of the fifth chapter of Matthew's account of the Gospel states, "And seeing the multitudes, he went you into a mountain and when he was set, his disciples came unto him." In this account of the Gospel, Jesus had just been baptized by John the Baptist, he had just conquered successfully the temptations in the Judean wilderness experience, and he has announced and begun his public ministry by calling disciples, preaching in the synagogues of Jerusalem, and healing the sick. As a matter of fact, Matthew 4:23-25 states, "Jesus was going throughout all Galilee, teaching in their synagogues and proclaiming the gospel of the kingdom, and healing every kind of disease and every kind of sickness among the people. The news about Him spread throughout all Syria; and they brought to Him all who were ill, those suffering with various diseases and pains, demoniacs, epileptics, paralytics; and He healed them. Large crowds followed Him from Galilee and the Decapolis and Jerusalem and Judea and from beyond the Jordan." That is how the fourth chapter of Matthew ends, and the fifth chapter opens with these words, "And seeing the multitudes...."

The Word of God is deliberate in all things. There is a message that you should grasp in the deliberate use of the word "multitudes or crowds" compared to "multitude or crowd." I want to suggest to you that a person will never come to the point of mourning over his or her personal sins sincerely and genuinely neither experience the promised comfort of Jesus if you are in the wrong crowd. If Matthew would have used the word multitude or crowd, it would have suggested a great number of people with one common purpose. But he didn't. Matthew is inspired to write, "And seeing the multitudes....", which suggests not one, but there were at least two great gatherings of people, with each group have its own common purpose.

As Jesus went about teaching and preaching and healing every manner of sickness and diseases, news about him spread like wildfire. People in need of a physical healing were brought to Jesus from at least five different regions—including from the other side of the Jordan River. But, when Jesus saw the multitudes or the crowds, He went up to a mountain and then His disciples came to Him. In these crowds was a group of people who were eager to learn from Him. But sadly, there was also a group who was only trying to receive a healing. If you are only following Jesus to receive tangible blessings from Him, you will never come to the point of seeing yourself for who you really are.

When you look at the end of the earthly life and ministry of Jesus and notice that after three years of having multitudes pressing Him, and multitudes following Him, the Apostle Luke tells us in the book of Acts that there were only one hundred and twenty disciples gathered together waiting on the promised coming of the Holy Spirit—after the resurrection and ascension of Jesus. Don't let a crowd fool you—everybody is not seeking the same thing or after the same thing from God! Many in the crowds or multitudes have mixed up priorities. That is why Jesus is recorded by Matthew a little further in this great Sermon on the Mount as saying, "But seek first His kingdom and His righteousness, and all these things will be added to you." (Matthew 6:33).

"And seeing the multitude..." In this portion of the quoted verse, it is important to know and understand that the word "seeing" in its original context literally means more than just looking. But— the word "seeing" more precisely and specifically means to know by observing. It means to gain some knowledge by watching. And as Jesus looks on this crowd, there are two things He readily observed. First, He knew that some people were only following Him to receive a healing. Secondly, Jesus knew what they were asking for or what they were seeking or waiting for was not what they really needed. In Jesus observing this crowd, He makes a clear distinction between needs and wants. They were asking for blinded eyes to be opened, but Jesus knew they really needed to open the eyes of their hearts. They were seeking for deafened ears to be unstopped, but Jesus knew the really needed to have the deafness of their souls removed. They were waiting for the manifestation of physical healings, but Jesus observes this crowd and knew they really needed spiritual healing.

As Jesus observes this great multitude, He saw just how messed up this crowd was and declared, "Blessed are the poor in spirit..... Blessed are they that mourn."

When you see yourself as Jesus sees you—when you see just how sinful you are, just how messed up you are, just how bad you have been, and just how wrong you are—it will make you mourn over the personal baggage and sin issues that are present in your life.

David did. The story of David, the King of Israel, reveals to us that even a man after God's own heart can become entrapped and entangled in the bondage of sin. David lusted for Bathsheba (who was bathing on a roof top in sight of the king's palace), he desired and did have an affair with Bathsheba. Bathsheba becomes pregnant and David attempts to cover up the fact that he is the father by having

Bathsheba's husband (Uriah) return from the warfront, entices him to become drunk with wine (for the purpose that Uriah would have sex with his wife). Uriah refuses to sleep with his wife, even while on furlough, because his fellow soldiers could not enjoy such pleasures while on the battlefield. Seeing that his plan had backfired, David then plots to have Uriah killed when he returns to battle, and then David takes Bathsheba into his house as his own wife. Despite the many acts of sin committed by David, it wasn't until his conversation with the prophet Nathan that David fully realized how sinful he had become and he really "saw himself." It was at this exposition of his dirty laundry, and seeing who he had become, that David mourned, moaned, and grieved over his sins, repented and cried out, "Create in me a clean heart, O God, and renew a steadfast spirit within me. Do not cast me away from your presence, and do not take away your Holy Spirit from me. Restore to me the joy of your salvation" (Psalm 51:10-12).

When you see yourself as Jesus sees you—when you see just how sinful you are, just how messed up you are, just how bad you have been, and just how wrong you are—it will make you mourn over the personal baggage and sin issues that are present in your life.

The publican did. In the parable of the Pharisee and the Publican as recorded in Luke 18 at the hour of prayer, the Pharisee was trusting in himself, he was self-righteous, and had a contempt for others and viewed himself as superior or better than others. However, the publican, this tax-collector who made his living by swindling and cheating others, in his time of prayer he could not even lift his eyes to heaven—because he was so shameful, and he beat his chest (which was a symbol and outward expression of sorrow, mourning and grief). And as he prayed, he reflected over all the acts sin and the wrong he had done, and then he cried out, "God be merciful to me, the sinner!"

When you see yourself as Jesus sees you—when you see just how sinful you are, just how messed up you are, just how bad you have been, and just how wrong you are—it will make you mourn over the personal baggage and sin issues that are present in your life.

The Apostle Paul did. This great evangelist, this great preacher, this great theologian and promoter of the early church was not all that great in his life before he met Jesus Christ on the Damascus Road. In the book of Romans, as Paul was reflecting over his former life as a persecutor and murderer of those who were following the way of Jesus Christ, and even reflected over the struggles that were present in his saved life. And after these reflections and scenes of realities had flashed before his eyes, the Apostle Paul even cried out, "O wretched man that I am!"

You just have to really look at yourself.

The late Michael Jackson, the great icon of Pop Music, once recorded a song in which we are all challenged to pull out a mirror and take a good look at ourselves. A portion of the lyrics to the song, *Man In The Mirror*, states, "I am looking at the man in the mirror, and I am asking him to change his ways. No message could have been any clearer, if you want to make the world a better place, take a look at yourself, and then make a change."

There are many people who know they are living life in the wrong, they know they have a history or a pattern of making mistakes—but they are pretending to be right. However, true blessedness begins with deep sadness. There is joy through mourning. There is freedom through surrender. There is liberty through confession. But, in order to begin the process of experiencing this blissful blessedness, a person must come to point of acknowledging that he has messed up, fallen short, sinned and acted in a dishonorable way and manner in his life. In other words, after you look back over the faults and failures that you have committed within your life, you can then utter and express the same mournful cry given by the Apostle Paul, "O, wretched man that I am!" (Romans 7:24). If you can honestly have that as your own personal plea and cry, then you are on your way to experience the blessings of God. Because true blessedness begins with a deep sadness.

When You Truly See Yourself As Jesus Sees You—You Will Be Comforted

The word "comforted" has such a deep, special meaning. This word literally means to be called near to or to invite. It gives the idea that once a person realizes that he or she is spiritually dead, you will genuinely begin to grieve over your spiritual separation from God— God, in return, honors your admission of destitution and fills the spiritual void in your life by calling you near to Him through His son, Jesus the Christ.

And, this comfort of Jesus is a settled peace, it is a sweet relief, it is a sweet consolation within. This comfort of Jesus is an assurance of forgiveness, it is an acceptance by God, and it is a sense of God's presence and His care just for you!

When you mourn over your sinful state and position, you are then called or invited to share in the power of forgiveness, restoration and reconciliation provided through the resurrection of Jesus Christ.

One of the greatest privileges I personally have in this life is to be the father of five beautiful children. They are not perfect, they make mistakes like all of us—but they are still beautiful in my eye-sight. And, one of the responsibilities, privileges, and benefits of fatherhood is to be able to comfort your child or children. When my children feel hurt, I tell them just how special and unique they are. When my children are injured, I do whatever it takes to make them feel better. I call them nearer to me. I invite them into the presence of my extended and opened arms.

There is a story that is told of a father who was so overjoyed at the birth of his baby boy. He and his wife were thrilled to be parents of a six-year old daughter. But, now he just experienced the birth of his son—his name sake. The father was so overjoyed, that it pained his heart to hear and see his son cry. It pained him so much, that every time the baby cried he would run into the nursery, pick him up from his crib and hold him within his arms. His wife, became very deeply concerned that her husband was going to spoil the baby by picking him up every time he cried. So, she said to her husband, "You need to stop picking the baby up every time he cries. You are going to spoil him. You have to promise me that you are going break that habit." Reluctantly, the father promised his wife. One day, in the absence of his wife, the baby started crying and he would not stop. The father tried to feed the baby, but he was not hungry. He checked his diaper, but it was dry. The baby kept crying because he wanted to be held and taken out of the crib. The father reached down to pick up his crying son. Just then, his daughter came into the nursery and said, "Daddy, you can't pick the baby up. Mommy said, you can't pick him up every time he cries." The father laid his son back down in the crib. Looked at his daughter and said, "I forgot. I did promise your mother that I would not pick the baby up every time he cries." But the baby was still crying—this time louder than before. The father wanted to comfort his son in an extreme way, and then he smiled. He looked at his little girl and said, "I promised your mother I would not pick him up, but I never promised her that I would not climb into the crib with him." So, he climbed into that crib, laid beside his son and comforted and re-assured his new born baby.

Please understand that there is a Heavenly Father who can comfort you like no one else can. There is a father who will hold you until you are better. There is a father who can help you until you can live with the hurt being experienced in your life. There is a father who will walk with you until the end, who will be with you in the midnight hours of your life, and who will look beyond all of your faults and see your many needs.

Thank you God, for being our father who comforts!

Chapter 3
Blessed Are The Meek

The word "meek" is one of the most misunderstood words in the English language and one of the most misunderstood biblical characteristics of a godly person. I want to suggest that the modern day application and definition for meekness has severely harmed or endangered the original intention and meaning of the word.

For many in today's culture, the word meek is usually attributed or associated with weakness. This once honorable word now carries with it the idea of spinelessness, and individual bowing in cowardice to others, or an ineffective, weak, and timid individual.

Although, many have mistakenly and falsely added a weak connotation, description or meaning to the word(s) "meek or meekness", there really is so much great strengthen associated with this word. Literally, the word means to have a strong, but tender and humble life. A person who is characterized as being meek has a strong, yet teachable spirit. It was Aristotle, that great Greek scholar, who defined meekness as the means between excessive anger and excessive *"angerlessness."* In other words, to Aristotle, meekness is that happy medium between too much anger and too little anger. If I could surmise, I would suggest that Aristotle's translation of the first part of Matthew 5:5 would be something like this, "Blessed is the man who is always angry at the right time and never angry at the wrong time."

But, then the Greek word (*praus*) translated into meekness has an additional meaning to it as well. It was primarily used as the word for a wild animal which has been domesticated...an animal which has been trained to obey the word of command from it's master. It is the word for an animal which has learned to accept control. Therefore, this verse could easily be translated, "Blessed is the man who has every instinct, every impulse, and every passion under control. Blessed is the man who is entirely-self controlled."

This one word, "meek", suggests to us the tremendous, insurmountable amount of strength we have to control ourselves in what would seem like uncontrollable situations. In other words, as a born-again believer—you don't have to act a plumb fool while facing negative situations in this life. A few years back, there was a very popular rap song recorded, and the lyrics relay the impression of the songwriter not handling the pressures of life well. In the course of that song, the rapper exclaims, "Y'all gonna make me lose my mind up in here, up in here......Y'all gonna make me act a fool up in here, up in here...." But as we look at this section of the Sermon on the Mount, we will soon discover that you don't have to lose your mind and you don't have to act a fool, if you are a spiritually meek person.

The progression of this Sermon on the Mount suggests that you are able to be domesticated and tamed because of the presence of the Spirit of God dwelling within you. After you realize just how poor in spirit you are, and after you have finished mourning over your spiritual destitution, Jesus then gives us the promise of being filled and comforted.

"Blessed are the poor in spirit, for they shall be filled. Blessed are they that mourn, for they shall be comforted." The words "filled" and "comforted" are also used in association with the Holy Spirit. I understand and know that there are people, situations and circumstances in your life which will make you want to act out of character. But God lets us know that we can remain in control of our emotions and actions by the aide and the assistance of the Holy Spirit—if we would only remember that He is in control. However, as I survey the actions of some believers in the body of Christ and their mannerisms and actions within our churches, I am become a firmer believer by the day that our churches are still filled a few people who act just like "undomesticated animals." A quick study or review of the animal kingdom would teach us or remind us that it's difficult to keep or to raise a wild or undomesticated animal with a tamed or domesticated animal. When attempts are made to raise the undomesticated with the domesticated, generally it will produce or generate chaos and havoc in the environment. However, for the person who is tamed or domesticated by the Holy Spirit....when you feel like striking back, you will turn the other cheek....when you feel like using words with an obscene overtone, you will refrain and bless the offending person with kind words instead....when you feel like fighting, you will lift holy hands in praise.

So, if a restrained lifestyle is a blessing reserved for the meek, the question that needs to be asked and answered is, "Who are the meek?" The meek is the person who is humble, and not prideful. The meek is the one who is gentle in spirit, and not easily provoked. The meek is the one who is forgiving, and not revengeful. The meek are the ones who are controlled, and not living an undisciplined like.

As we look at this verse, some twenty-one centuries later after Jesus first uttered these words, what is this verse saying to us today? How can we apply this verse to our lives? I want to suggest to us that this verse is important for one major reason. The sad indictment today is that many Christians are guilty of allowing negative situations and conditions being experienced in life to master them, instead of them mastering the situations and conditions. When you allow things in this life to master you, and you respond in an unrestrained, uncontrollable manner, you are prone to do unusual things to get back ahead of the curve. Unusual things such as selling your body, dope, crack and smack. Unusual things such as stealing from your own parents or grandparents. Unusual things such as compromising godly teachings and principles you once reverently and strongly believed and followed—just to get ahead of the game again.

Understanding What It Meant To Be Meek In the First Century

I must admit, there is no greater struggle one has than to continue to do the right thing in the face of so much injustice. Yet, the expectation from God is that we are to remain in self-control.

On that day when Jesus began teaching his disciples, there was such an increasing and growing crowd, that he went up on the mountain to teach and to be seen. During this time of history, the people of Jerusalem were experiencing so much injustice in the land. Their land, the promised land of Canaan, was no longer their own. It's a terrible thing to be able to live in a land that God had promised you, but yet in reality, it doesn't belong to you. Jerusalem and the region of Palestine were now under the authority of the Roman Empire. Secondly, the injustice being experienced by the Jewish people was expressed in their forced obligation to pay significant taxes to the Caesar of Rome. Also, this particular form of injustice was even more complicated through the practice of the Romans hiring Jewish people to collect taxes from their own people, and then padding the tax bill in the process to support their own livelihood. Even the social structure of the Jewish culture was impartial. The upper class of the Jewish people were exploiting, abusing or taking advantage of those who were associated with a lower social status. In other words, the spirit of looking out for your brother, or being your brother's keeper, was not being practiced in that day and culture. So, as Jesus sees this multitude, he sees this crowd.....knowing all of the acts of injustice, knowing all about the social ills and the wrongs within that culture during that day and time. But yet, he cried out, "Blessed are the meek." Blessed are the ones who hold back their wrath. Blessed are the ones who don't take matters into their own hands. Blessed are the ones who don't act out or against their godly character.

That is a brief picture of the climate during the earthly days of Jesus when he gives this sermon. However, forty years later, the climate didn't get any better—if anything, the situations grew worse. It wasn't until forty years after the death of Jesus, when God, through the inspiration of the Holy Spirit, moved upon the heart of Matthew (who is a transformed or changed former tax collector) to write this letter of good news about a suffering, yet victorious, savior who lived, died and reclaimed his life on the third appointed morning. A little more than forty years later, Matthew writes the gospel message of Jesus to give encouragement, strength and hope to the suffering Jewish-Christians at Jerusalem. The opposition in their lives had intensified, as evidenced by the greater strain of the tension between the Jews and Christians, the ongoing presence of the social ills, the Roman Empire had just unleashed a massive war of destruction against Jerusalem, the city had been destroyed by fire, the temple of God had been destroyed, and Christians were literally being killed by the authority of the Roman government. They were having to endure perplexing perils of persecution. But in the midst of it all, Matthew is reminded of the words of Jesus and is inspired to include this account of Jesus' teaching and ministry in his letter of encouragement to the suffering saints in Jerusalem and echoes the words of Jesus, "Blessed are the meek."

Understanding What It Means To Be Meek In The Twenty-First Century

Listening to the words of Jesus in the face of what was happening in the first century would seem to be hard to do. As a matter of fact, listening to words of Jesus, in the face of the social ills and injustices in the twenty-first century is hard to do. But, those same words spoken by Jesus are still echoing in our ears today, "Blessed are the meek."

In this great Sermon on the Mount, it appears as if Jesus quotes verse eleven of the thirty-seventh Psalm, "But the humble (meek) will inherit the land and will delight themselves in abundant prosperity." When you read the beginning verses of this psalm and see such verses and words as, "Do not fret because of evildoers, be not envious toward wrongdoers. For they will wither quickly like the grass and fade like the green herb" (Psalm 37:1-2), it reminds you that there is no secret that the times in which we live are perilous and treacherous times, where the wicked are seemingly prospering and the people of

God are constantly suffering. As you look at the conditions and the signs of the time today, there are many problems that have to be endured. Socially there are problems. There are still wars and rumors of wars. Famine is still rampant within our land and throughout the world. Crime is at an all time high, and moral degradation is rampant. Economically there are problems. Social Security is no longer secure. There are major corporate financial and Wall Street scandals appearing every few months. Many individuals have invested thirty years of their working lives on one job, only to discover that a crooked management team has robbed them of their retirement funds. The rich are still getting richer at the expense and demise of an eroding middle class and an ever growing lower class. Even within the realms of religion, there are problems. Christian boldness is virtually non-existent. Fifty years ago, the Supreme Court made a ruling to remove prayer from our schools. An increasing and growing number of people in this age and time are coming to the opinion and belief in the non-existence of God. And morally, our modern-day society is acting as if they don't have a conscious or a sense of public responsibility.

We are living in the midst of perilous times. However, the sad part about is the fact that many within the Christian faith really don't know how to cope or live a godly life during this age. Many Christians are not adequately equipped or prepared to live a pleasing life to God in such perilous times. I contend that as the world grows more wicked and wiser, it seems to me that we, as Christians, are as well. Many of us are failing to live the "transformed life" that Paul encourages us to live in Romans 12:2. Seemingly, it appears that more and more we are conforming to the world's standards. One reason for this is, just possibly, because we often build up a false illusion that life as a believer in Christ is liking living full-time in a rose garden. We fail to teach new babes in Christ that roses have thorns on them. We have to constantly remind ourselves exactly what Jesus taught his disciples, and that is that life for a Christian will not find you living on easy street every day. Jesus said, "In this world you will have tribulation" (John 16:33). The reality is that in this life....we will be up sometimes, and down sometimes; we can be in the valley today, and living on the mountainside tomorrow; there will be bright sunshine one day, followed by gloomy skies the next. In other words, the conditions we often find ourselves living in, these perilous times we all find ourselves facing periodically in life, can prompt and prime us to be a living portrayal of a line found in a song recorded by Marvin Gaye, these conditions in this life "will make you want to holler and through up both of your hands."

However, there is some consolation and hope found in the 37th Psalm. In this psalm you will soon discover that trouble won't last always. In this psalm, the psalmist speaks of two adversaries—evildoers and workers of iniquity. Also, in this psalm there is a warning to the household of faith—and that is to fret not and don't become envious. In the life of this psalm we see two sets of people who we personally have a hard time dealing with in our own lives. For the majority of us, we don't know how to deal with evildoers, and we don't know how to handle workers of iniquity. The Hebrew word for evildoers literally means an individual who "spoils by breaking into pieces." In other words, it is an individual whose personal intention is to take from you by tearing something up in your life. Evildoers will lie on you, persecute you, criticize you and intentionally seek to destroy you. Evildoers will call you every name in the book but a child of God. And when these evildoers are present in your life, and you are faced with these periods of opposition and strife, many times you are tempted to fret when you shouldn't. When the evildoers are present in your life, you begin to wring your hand in worry, your nerves become agitated and troubled, and some just fly completely off the handle and lose all sense of identity as being a child of God.

Likewise, the psalmist issues or gives a warning about becoming envious of the workers of iniquity. The workers of iniquity are those who prosper through ill-gotten gains. Many times when we look at these individuals and their outward appearances of success and perceived blessings, sometimes it causes us to scratch our heads in wonder and we just can't understand why. The workers of iniquity drive the finest cars, have the biggest roll of money you will ever see, they flourish and prosper, they experience all of their desires, they do what they want to do, and they give the illusion (as false as it may be) that they are living life in ease, fat, large and in charge. And here it is, you look at the reality of your life—you give your tithes and offerings to God cheerfully and with great joy, you work faithfully in striving to advance the kingdom of God, and it seems like you just can't prosper or get ahead in life.

If we are not careful in our thoughts and guarding our hearts, we will be tempted to act just like the evildoers and the workers of iniquity in order to get ahead. That is why the psalmist issues the warning and said, "Do not fret....and be not envious." The consolation is knowing that evildoers and workers of iniquity will soon be cut down by the coming judgment of our God. Their triumphing is short. But unless they repent, their weeping and wailing will be everlasting.

That is the fate of their reality. But the question for us becomes, "What do you do in the meantime?"

We hear God promising that perilous times will not last always, but what do we do between verses one and two in the 37th Psalm? How do we make it through this holding pattern so many of us have found ourselves in?

When you read verses through eleven of this psalm, the psalmist said the first thing we have to do is to maintain our trust in the Lord. In other words, you have to learn how to grow and mature to the point that you can literally take God at His word.

When you look at the negative situations that are present in your life, and when you focus on the persecution that you have to endure, and then you turn again to see how the wicked are prospering—this conflicting view makes the conditions right or ripe for anyone to develop the thought to forsake or give up on God. It is at this moment when you are looking at conflicting views of the status of life between the righteous and the unrighteous that you have to diligently maintain your trust in God. When it seems as if you can't understand why God would allow His children to go through and experience certain negative situations in life—you still must trust Him.

One of the older saints of my home church, the late Mother Gladys Carothers, use to say, "Baby, you gotta trust God for one thing, and trust Him for all." You may not understand God, but keep your trust in Him. By trusting in God, we are demonstrating our faith in Him, as well as we are demonstrating our faith in His divine care for us. There is a story that is told of a mother who would always struggle with her little boy when it was time to wash his hair. The mother would thoroughly wet and lather his hair. But when it was time for the rinse, the little boy would always squirm and become anxious, because the suds would run down into his face and burn his eyes. And his mother would always tell him, "Son, just trust me. Keep your head up, and the suds will not run down your face and burn your eyes." When I thought about that story, I realized that for many of us our relationship with God is so similar. I know that God is our Father. I know that He loves each and every one of us. I believe that most of us do trust Him. But, sometimes in an extremely difficult situation we panic and turn our eyes away from Him—and this never solves the problem. Our turning away makes us more afraid as "the shampoo" blinds us. Although the son knew that his mother loved him, he had a difficult time trusting her in his panicky situation. The mother knew she could protect him, but convincing the little boy was not easy, especially when all he could feel was water coming down his face. His lack of trust hurt his mother, but it hurt the little boy even more (he was the one who had to suffer through burning eyes). Likewise, I am sure that our lack of trust hurts God, but it hurts us even more.

Often in the Bible we are told to lift up our heads when problems come into our lives. We lift them up, because God loves us and can protect us. So the next time you are in the bathtub of life, and water and shampoo begin to run down your face....JUST LIFT YOUR HEAD UP! The Bible declares and states with an emphatic question, "I will lift up my eyes to the hills; for where shall my help come?" (Psalm 121:1).

Not only must maintain our trust in the Lord, but then the psalmist said we must delight ourselves in Him as well. To delight yourself in the Lord is to desire and enjoy the nearness of His presence and the truth and righteousness of His word. In the midst of living with losses in your life—the loss of loved ones, the loss of prosperity, the loss of relationships, whatever it may be—you have to remember that nobody can do you like Jesus can. Delight yourself in the goodness of God during the times of your gloom.

If you can do this, then you will realize the promise of restoration just for you, "Delight yourself in the Lord, and God will give you the desires of your heart" (Psalm 37:4). Jesus said this way, "But seek ye first the kingdom of God and His righteousness, and all these things will be added unto you" (Matthew 6:33).

Not only must you trust God and delight yourself in Him, but you also must commit your way to Him. A person who is to be blessed by God must totally turn his or her life over to God. We must make God our supreme guide and submit in everything to His guidance and disposal. If you really want to persevere through your perilous times, then you must offer your ways to the Lord and not to the world's standards. However, an offering does not really transpire, occur or happen if your hands are still holding on to what is being offered. I implore you to learn how to take your hands off of your life and commit it totally to Jesus. Learn how to live out the words of that beloved hymn of commitment, "All to Jesus I surrender. All to Him I freely give. I surrender all. I surrender all. All to thee my blessed savior, I surrender all."

In this discussion of learning how to live in this life by restraining ourselves with a meek spirit, not only must we trust God, delight ourselves in Him, and commit our total being to God, but the psalmist also says we have to learn how rest in the Lord and wait patiently for Him. The word "rest" in this connotation means to set one's mind at ease. The words to an old Negro spiritual reflects this thought as its lyrics gives a description of what it means to rest in the Lord, "I woke up this morning with my mind stayed on Jesus." Wherever your focal point is in this life, that is where you will find the source of your comfort and consolation. If you desire and want some dependable comfort and consolation in this life, you must find yourself resting in the Lord. You have to take total refuge and find a sweet solace in the arms of the Lord. Once you have done this, and the Lord becomes your safe haven, shelter, and sanctuary—fasten your seat belt and wait patiently for God to move.

I understand that waiting is one of the hardest and most difficult things for us to do, but please learn to keep waiting for the move of God in your life. When you feel like giving up, just wait on God. When you feel like giving in, just wait on Him. When you are just about ready to throw in the towel, give up on life, or preparing to handle the situation yourself in a worldly manner, just wait on God. For the biblical record and promise is that there is a blessing in waiting on God. Isaiah say, "Has thou not known? Has thou not heard that the everlasting God, the Lord the creator of the ends of the earth fainteth not, neither is he weary? There is no searching of his understanding. He gives power to the faint, and to them who have no might, he increases their strength. Even the youth shall faint and be weary, and the young men shall utterly fall. But they that wait on the Lord shall renew their strength, they shall mount up with wings like an eagle, they shall run and not weary, they shall walk and not faint" (Isaiah 40:08-31).

Yes, there is a blessing in waiting. So, keep waiting—you can make it. You might be weeping now, but joy will come in the morning. You may be crying now, but God will wipe away every tear. It may be dark in your life now, but there is a bright side somewhere. You may be broke, busted and disgusted now, but pay day is coming your way.

Again, notice the words of Jesus, "Blessed are the meek, for they shall inherit the earth." To the Jews in the first century, the words of Jesus was good news. There was mass destruction in their promised land. The Romans had taken authority and reign of their promised land. But hearing Jesus speak that day, He promised and assured them that they would get it all back.

As a practical application for you, I don't know what you may have lost, but this verse should remind you that you can get it all back. Just stand still. Hold your peace. Bridle your tongues. Guard your heart, mind and words. Protect and preserve your character and reputation as a child of God, and you will receive your lost possessions.

Chapter 4
Blessed Are They Which Do Hunger And Thirst After Righteousness

Hunger and thirst. Jesus uses two physical descriptions regarding one's bodily needs in order to make a point of perplexity followed by potential promises in relation to our spirituality with God. However, many of us don't experience the reality of this promised in our lives because we don't have appreciation and understanding of the perplexing point or problem in the physical sense. The fact is that very few of us in our modern conditions of life know what it really means to be hungry or thirsty (physically). However, in the days and the world of the historical Jesus it was a totally different story. In the first century, a working man's wage was the equivalent of fourteen cents. Even making every possible effort for the difference in the purchasing power of money from the 21st century to the 1st century, no man, or woman, or family could live comfortably on fourteen cents a day.

A working man and his family in Palestine ate meat only once a week. In Palestine during the first century, the working man and the day laborer were never far from the border line of real hunger and starvation. It was the same way with thirstiness. It was not possible for the vast majority of people to turn on a faucet or a tap and fine clear, cold running water coming into the house. As they journeyed, moved, lived and traveled in desert like conditions—with the hot sun beating down on them, the hot wind blowing in their faces blowing dry, steamy sand into their nostrils, so much to the point whereas they would cover their faces with scarves because of the feeling that the combination of the hot wind and the dry sand would suffocate them. Their throats would naturally of course be dry, with no means (no water or other liquids) to quench their thirsty desire.

In our culture, we really have no comparison to that at all. We really don't know what it means to be hungry, and we really don't know what it means to be thirsty. Not in the physical sense. And sadly, not in relation to our spirituality either. In today's culture we have weakened, crippled, and almost destroyed our hunger and thirstiness for God. For example, in our culture today, we can attend worship when worship fits "our" schedule (8:00 am, 9:00 am, 11:00 am or 6:00 pm on Sundays, Tuesday night, Wednesday at noon, Wednesday at 6:00 pm, or Saturday night worship). In today's culture, we can stay home, turn the television on at any time of the day and our "Word" in. If we miss church on a particular Sunday, we can go to a church's website at our luxury and convenience. You can click this tab to hear the sermon, click another tab to hear the choir sing, click a third tab to read the announcements and make one final click to give a tithe by credit card. In our attempts to make church convenient, I am afraid that we have eroded the populace's hunger and thirst for God. It is sad, but church today has to be flexible. Our churches today have to compete with the rest of the world for individual's time demands.

So, then the question becomes, as we look at this particular Beatitude, "How much do you want righteousness?" How deeply do you want to do the right thing, and have the right relationship with God? Do you want it as much as a starving man want bread? Do you want it as much as a dying man wants water? To hunger and thirst after righteousness literally means to have a starving spirit. It is possessing real hunger and starvation for the soul.

Jesus gives the promised of a filled life; however, most of us are on a quest of wanting our lives filled. And in our quest of fulfilling this desire, many times we are guilty of running ourselves crazy, spinning our wheels only to go nowhere fast, trying to fulfill it ourselves, and yet Jesus has already given us the promise that He would do it for us. However, it is a conditional promise. Jesus promised that we would be filled or satisfied only after we have a sincere hunger and thirstiness for the righteousness of God. This promise is similar to the teachings of Jesus as he gives it in Matthew 6:33. The promise is similar, and likewise the problem is similar as well. In Matthew 6:33, Jesus promised that "these things" will be added to our lives, after we have first the kingdom of God and His righteousness. But the problem is that many are still making "these things" a priority over God, rather than making God a priority over "these things."

In looking at this particular Beatitude, it's tone takes my mind back to the words of the psalmist David as recorded in Psalm 42:1-2. David said, "As the deer pants after the water brooks, so pants my soul after You, O God. My soul thirsts for God, for the living God."

In their hey days, the rock band known as the Rolling Stones recorded a song entitled, *I Can't Get No Satisfaction.* The basis or the theme of this song centers around a man who is in search for something or someone in this world to satisfy or fill an emptiness or void in his life. I must admit that I am a little too young to remember all of the lyrics to the song. But I do remember that this man had finally gotten to the point where he realized that nothing or no one could satisfy him, and that nothing or no one could make him happy. He had tried everything and everyone he could think of to satisfy him. As a matter of fact, a very popular line in that song has the man crying out and saying, "I have tried, and I have tried, and I have tried, but I just can't get no satisfaction." As you look at this 42nd Psalm, I want you to see that in essence David was living in this same state and situation. As we hear David cry out in this psalm, it is as if he is saying, "I can't get no satisfaction."

In looking at the background of the 42nd Psalm, we see a David who is running from the hands of his own son, Absalom. Absalom has revolted against his own father. He is at the point that if could just get his hands on David—who is his father and the king of Israel—

he would surely kill him. Absalom has driven David from his palace, from the city of Jerusalem, and from the sanctuary of the temple of God. David pens or writes this psalm because of the way he is feeling since he has been banished from the tabernacle of God, the place of worship.

David has been banished. I understand that "banish" is a strong word for me to use to describe David's feelings. But it literally means not being allowed to do something. It means that something has been cut off, removed or eliminated from your very presence and or privilege. And what has been removed from David's life is the place of worship. There are so many people who are just like David in our communities, our homes, and even in our churches. People who have been banished from the place of worship. You see, what ultimately banished David from the tabernacle was sin. And, what ultimately allows us to banish ourselves from the place of worship is our own sin.

The book of 2 Samuel, in particular the 11th and 12th chapters, reveal to us the sin David had committed is ultimately the reason for his fleeing from Absalom. David sinned when he had an affair with Bathsheba. David sinned when he had Uriah, Bathsheba's husband killed in order to cover up her pregnancy by him. The Bible does state that David did acknowledge his sin before God. He did repent of his sin. We even hear his repented prayer and cry, "Lord create within me a clean heart, renew within me the right spirit, and restore unto me the joy of my salvation." David was forgiven of his sins by God—this is evidenced by the prophet Nathan's statement to David that the Lord has put away his sins (2 Samuel 12:13). He was forgiven by God, but Nathan also reminded David that he would still be chastised by God. Nathan told David that the sword would never leave his house. In other words, he reminded David that he would still experience storms, due to his sin, even though he had been forgiven. And that is what we see in the life of this text—we see a sword in the hands of Absalom, and David has been banished from the sanctuary of God. David had to run in order to save his own life. He had to leave Jerusalem, which also meant he would not be able to enjoy the worship experience in the tabernacle or the sanctuary devoted to God. Ultimately, he is running from Absalom because of the consequences of sin which was present in his life.

As a point of practical application for us today, acknowledging our faults and sins should make us run. But the problem is that many of us are running in the wrong direction. Instead of our running towards God, instead of running towards the house of God, many people run away from God and His sanctuary. We banish ourselves. We attempt to remove ourselves from the presence of God. We take ourselves away from the house of God. You see, many of us have the wrong idea and concept about sin, acknowledging sin, and being forgiven of our sin. Nowhere in the Bible do you find any teachings about staying away from the place of worship when sin is present in your life. However, many come to the point of acknowledging they have sinned, and have even asked God to forgive them, but will still allow guilt to enter their hearts, and will allow a feeling of unworthiness to enter their minds. These two factors, guilt and the feeling of unworthiness, ought to be present in your heart and mind before you ask God to forgive you, which leads you to point of seeking and asking for forgiveness. But once we have been forgiven, the feelings of guilt and unworthiness should not be in our hearts and minds, which becomes a strong catalyst to cause you to keep you from the sanctuary of God.

You have to constantly remind yourself that no one is worthy. We all have sinned. We all have come short of the glory of God. We are all sinners. We are all wretches undone. If you or someone you know has banished himself from the house of the Lord, remind him (or yourself) that yes, you or he ought to be running—but you need to make sure you are running towards God and not away from Him.

God wants us to turn to him in order to receive help and strength. How many of you will experience severe sickness and purposefully run away from the hospital? How many of you, if you are about to run out of gas, the hand of the gas gauge is already past empty, would intentionally drive past the nearest gas station? You need to realize that when sin is present in your life that you must run towards God. For God and God alone is our refuge and our strength. For God is a very present help in times of trouble. But, when we banish ourselves from the temple, we never have a state of being filled, we never have a state of being satisfied. When we remove ourselves from the very presence of God, never do we reach the point of satisfaction in our lives

Many have banished themselves from God, from the place of worship and have sought satisfaction from other resources of this world. They have sought satisfaction from the liquor crowd, which told them to drink their way out. They have sought satisfaction from drug dealers and dope pushers, who told them to snort, smoke, and shoot their way out. Many have sought satisfaction from money and healthy bank accounts, which told them to buy their way out. They have sought satisfaction through jobs, careers and business that told them to work their way out. Some have even come to the point of throwing up both of their hands and cried, "There is no way out. I can't get no satisfaction. I have tried, and tried and tried. But, I just can't get no satisfaction."

But thanks be to the glory of God, that we can still find satisfaction in Jesus Christ! Because even now, over two thousand years after the life, death, burial and resurrection, we can still hear Jesus say, "I am the way, the truth and the life." There is a way out of your point of not having any satisfaction. If you have been trying the world's standards and ways and still can't find any satisfaction in this life, I want you to know that there is a way back to have a satisfied life.

God Still Sheds His Grace

The way back to having a satisfied life begins with you realizing that God still sheds His grace on us despite ourselves. What makes a deer run? A deer runs because it is being threatened as a hunted prey, or it runs because of the apparent threat of danger. The good news is the fact that the deer is panting lets us know that it's life has been spared. Whatever the imminent threat or danger was, it did not consume the now panting deer.

Likewise, many have committed so many acts that were displeasing in the eyesight of God. It was the combination of guilt and shame that caused us to run away from the arms of a forgiving God. But in the midst of our running away, God was still gracious towards us—as no harm has come. And, He is still gracious enough to you new mercies every day. Some have been in situations, in the midst of your running, that should have you locked behind jail cells, but God spared you just one more time. And, you need to understand and realize it's not that God is condoning the wrong you have done—He just loves us all so much that He sees our failures, forgives us of our sins, looks beyond our faults, shortcomings and our wrongs, and gives us another chance. That is nothing but grace.

Develop A Thirstiness For God

"As the deer pants for the water brooks, so my soul pants for You, O God" (Psalm 42:1). Barred from public worship. Banished from the place of public worship. David was heart sick! When you look at David and his desires in this particular psalm—he did not want to be delivered from his trouble, he was not seeking ease from his pains or problems, he was not after honor and glory. All David was seeking, desiring and wanting was the enjoyment of communing with God in the sanctuary.

David's soul had an urgent need of being with God. He viewed communion with God, not merely as a luxury, but rather he viewed it as an absolute necessity for his life—just like a water is essential for a running deer. Like a man lost in the desert, his canteen is empty and dry as a bone, but comes to a well and discovers that the well is dry. This man, who is lost in a dry desert, must discover water soon so he may drink and not die. In this psalm, David basically says, "I must have God or I will faint!" He said, "my soul", literally meaning his very self and being, the deepest part of who he is (his mind, his feelings, his will) needed a sense of the divine presence of God.

Look at the urgency of David's desire for communion with God. "My soul thirsts for God, for the living God." It has been well documented that for those who have gone on hunger strikes, for whatever the reason might be, an individual can live or exist for approximately one hundred days with no food, as long as you have excess to water. However, the same is not case for water. You can only last a few days without water. Thirstiness has a great urgency than hunger. David had an urgent need of wanting spiritual union with God in the tabernacle.

I understand that we can worship God anywhere and at anytime. I understand that one of the attributes or the characteristics of the nature of God is that He is omnipresent (everywhere present at the same time). However, there is still something special about meeting God in His sanctuary! There is something special about coming together and worshipping God in the place which was devoted, dedicated and consecrated to Him. That is why the writer of the book of Hebrews was inspired to write in that 10th chapter, "Let us consider one another in order to stir up loved and good works, not forsaking the assembling of ourselves together." I have to admit, that I don't understand and see how some people can come to God's house when they get good and ready. I don't understand how people can make it in life coming to worship one week, skipping two weeks, and then showing up again at Christmas and Easter. I understand it. The reason I can't understand is because when I, personally, am unable to make to public worship it feels like I am missing something. When I can't make it to the sanctuary, it feels like I am starving on the inside. There is something special about being in fellowship with God in His house. In God's house you will find love, joy, peace, deliverance, salvation, forgiveness, and the list can go on and on.

Many have been running in the streets doing this and that. You have been spared by the grace of God. Spared despite the fact of who you are and what you have done. After reading this psalm and beatitude, you ought to be running back to God with your tongue wagging just like a thirsty, tired dog, crying out, "If I don't taste of God.... drink of God....have fellowship with God, I will just die!"

In this psalm, David is saying that he had been accustomed to being in the sanctuary, and he asks the question as to when he would be restored to the privilege of again uniting with his people in public prayer and praise.

That is the question that was on David's mind. And that is the question that is on the minds of so many others—perhaps even you. And the answer is such a simple one. Stop running. It is all up to you.

Many are not in public worship with others because of the guilt of their past. If you have sincerely repented, and have asked God to forgive you, you can stop running right now and make your way back to the tabernacle! It's just that simple. Just know that all have sinned and come short of the glory of God.....but God is still standing with His arms wide opened. It's time to come back home!

So many people have tried to find satisfaction in this life separate of God, and separate from the sanctuary of God. As a personal testimony, I too tried finding satisfaction in the things and the people of this world. But then one day, I came to myself, as the prodigal son came to himself down in the hog pen, and I cried out, "I can't get no satisfaction. I have tried, and I have tried, but I can't get no satisfaction!"

But when I met God in His house, I became satisfied then! From that moment on, I have lived and experienced the words of the old hymn of the church, *"There is nothing so precious as Jesus is to me. Let earth with its treasures be gone. I am rich as can be, when my savior I see. I am happy with Jesus alone! I am happy with Jesus alone, O yes I am! I am happy with Jesus alone! Though poor and deserted, thank God I can say, I am happy with Jesus alone!"*

Chapter 5
Blessed Are The Merciful

In my first pastorate, the choir use to sing a song which included the following lyrics or line, "If everybody was like Jesus, what a wonderful world this would be." I use to love to hear that song, and would meditate and imagine on what could be. However, when I look at the actions, the thoughts and the desires as related to our own lives, and even the way some professed believers in Christ respond to the affairs of the church and hurting people in general, it makes me realize that we are far from a wonderful world.

We are not living out the true meaning of our status or position in Christ Jesus. We are called and carry the label of Christians—meaning we ought to be Christ-like.

On March 24, 1989, the worst oil spill in recorded history occurred off the coast of Alaska. Remember, it was the tanker ship called the Exxon Valdez which collided into the Bligh Reef, dumping more than 11 million gallons of crude oil into one of the most scenic and beautiful bodies of water in the world. Crude oil blackened or covered everything from the surface of the sea, to the beaches, to otters, to fish and to sea gulls. However, when I ponder over that great spill of oil in the Bligh Reef of Alaska, as terrible as this collision was, it was mild when compared to the collisions that occur daily in our relationships with one another. Many of us are guilty of not living out the true meaning of our name (Christians). A gospel song was recorded by a particular choir several years ago, and in this song the chorus line kept echoing and resonating the following words, "And they will know that we are Christians by our love." I am mighty afraid that many of us are only wearing the Christian title on our sleeves, but we are not living out the true meaning of our name.

After all, Jesus did give some truths on how to avoid collisions in our daily living with one another. Jesus said, "Love your enemy.... do good to those who misuse you....if they hit one cheek turn and let them hit the other one as well....if they ask for your coat, give them your cloak (or the clothes off your back) as well." However, when you look at our actions as professed people of God, it is evident that we are travelling on a collision path every day. We are called to be Christians, but too many people act like members of a church zoo. Some act like chameleons who are always changing their minds, thoughts, words, and actions with the changing of the crowd. Others act like roosters who are always crowing about something. Some act like goats as they are always butting somebody else. While others act gnats, as they are nothing but a pest in the lives of others. Some act like bumble bees—they have no problem in stinging anyone in their sight. Others act like cats and dogs as they just can't get along with one another. Some act like donkeys, as they are just plain stubborn and set in their ways. While others act like owls, always hooting about somebody when they are not around.

Look at the actions of some people. When someone doesn't meet their expectations, when promises go unfulfilled, it is not uncommon to find that verbal pistols are drawn and a round of words is fired. The result is nothing but a collision course of the heart. Many of us are guilty of walking around with a hole in our hearts. All the love of God has oozed out and the only thing you have left is bitterness and resentment. A part of your is broken, and the other part is bitter. A part of you wants to cry, and the other part wants to fight. If you are not careful, a fire of hatred will begin to burn in your heart. It's a blazing fire. It's a consuming fire. It's flames finally leap up as from a steaming pot of revenge.

At that moment, you are left with a decision. Do you put the fire out, or do you heat it up? Do you get over it, or do you get even? Do you release it, or do you resent it? Do you let your hurts heal, or do you allow your hurts to turn into hate? Are you left with decision, but I am afraid that many have made the wrong decision. This is evident in the fact that we have too many worldly-minded, worldly-acting and worldly-thinking people in our churches today. Many of our churches are infiltrated with worldly-acting Christians because of this bad-boy of a spirit named resentment. Let me share this with you about resentment. Resentment will take root in your life when you allow your hurt to manifest itself into hate. Resentment will manifest itself in your life when you allow what is eating at you to finally eat you up. Resentment will become prominent in your life when you poke, stoke, feed and fan the fire, stir the flames and constantly keep reliving that pain. Resentment is the deliberate decision to nurse the offense until it becomes a grudge in your life.

A Christian should never live with resentment and should never live without a merciful spirit towards one another.....especially since we have received so much from a merciful God!

The psalmist asked the question one day in the 116th Psalm, "What shall I render unto the Lord for all His benefits towards me?" In retrospect of that question asked by the psalmist, I have come to this one conclusion, it is a selfish person who has received so much from God and can't give it back! What have we received? We have received God's mercy, and we have also received God's grace! You see mercy and grace go hand in hand. The older saints didn't have much theological training. The older saints did not always have the opportunity to attend a bible college or a seminary. But, they knew something about the mercy and the grace of God. You could hear them simply saying, as they attempted to give a reasonable definition of the two, "Mercy is God holding back that which we do rightfully deserve, and grace is God giving us that which we don't deserve."

Grace and mercy go hand in hand!

In Genesis 19, God was preparing to destroy the wicked towns of Sodom and Gomorrah, but He sent His angels down to rescue Lot, his wife and family. When you look at this text, Lot responded to God's mercy in this way, "Now behold, your servant has found favor in your sight, and you have magnified your loving-kindness, which you have shown me by saving my life.." (Genesis 19:19).

The author of the book of Hebrews reminds us that grace and mercy go hand in hand. The Hebrew writer instructed the audience of his letter of just what type of advocate, intercessor, and High Priest we have in Jesus. In Hebrews 4:16 he said, "Therefore let us draw near with confidence to the throne of grace, so that we may receive mercy and find grace to help in time of need."

Even the great Mississippi Mass Choir reminds us in son that Mercy and Grace go hand in hand. The lyrics to a very popular song says, "Your grace and mercy have brought me through. I am living this moment because of you.....Justice demanded that I should die, but grace and mercy said, "Oh no, we have already paid the price!" Your grace and mercy have brought me through."

If and since we have received so much from God (His mercy and grace), why is then that too many Christians are living life with so much hell on the inside of them? Why do we have too many Christians living life with the cancer of revenge just eating away at them? Why do we have too many Christians living life with grudges taking up residence and residing in their hearts? Why do we have too many Christians living life with such unforgiving spirits? Why do we have too many Christians living life with a heart full of hatred, envy and jealousy?

We have to remember that we are called to reciprocate or reflect the very nature of God.

Merciful People Are Spirit Filled People

Look at the progression of this Sermon on the Mount. In the first four Beatitudes, you see a definite progression of spiritual awakening and transformation in the life of a believer. First, there is the discovery of the fact that I am nothing, I have nothing, and I can do nothing—there is a poverty of spirit. Secondly, there is the conviction of sin, a consciousness of guilt which produces godly sorrow—there is weeping and mourning. Next, there is a renouncing of self-dependence, a renouncing of the fact that you cannot save or deliver yourself—there is meekness. The fourth Beatitude suggests to us that after a renouncement of self-deliverance, there follows an intense longing for Christ and His salvation—there is hungering and thirsting after righteousness, with the promise of being filled.

I want to suggest to you that the first four Beatitudes describe how our lives are before Christ, and the next four Beatitudes describe how our lives should be or will be since Christ! A preview of the way life should be for a believer since salvation has come is found in this manner, "Blessed are the merciful.., blessed are the pure in heart..., blessed are the peacemakers..., blessed are those who are persecuted for righteousness sake..."

On this Christian journey, and on this railroad called life, if you ever run up against or cross paths with a professed Christian who is unmerciful, I strongly believe that the Word of God teaches that you might be encountering and unsaved individual! The Apostle John reminds us that the only way you can ever know if a person is actually saved or not is by looking at examining the quality of his or her heart. John said, "We know that we have passed out of death into life because we love the brethren. He who does not love abides in death" (I John 3:14). The word for "love" in this passage is *agape*, which carries the idea of unconditional and unmerited love. Our salvation is not evidenced in a charismatic gift, it is not solely evidenced in the things or the works we perform, it is not evidenced in our saying the right or correct spiritual things at all times. But it is evidenced in how well we love one another—especially our love for and towards other believers. A person cannot be a part of God's family and still have a heart filled with hatred. A person cannot be a part of the body of Christ and still have a heart consumed with grudges. A person cannot be a part of God's family and still maintain, possess or have a resentful spirit.

In order to be merciful—you must be saved. You must be spirit-filled.

Here is the clincher—God asked us not to judge one another (only judge ourselves). I understand that. I agree with that whole-heartedly. But the truth of the matter is, that when this self-examination period is over, it will still be evident that most of the hell-raisers in your church, on your job, and in your circle of family, friends, and acquaintances will stem from people living life with pinned up resentment, hatred and grudges in their hearts; and from people who don't have the spirit of God's love in their hearts.

The Merciful Are Compassionate And Forgiving People

The Greek word for merciful is *eleemones* (el-eh-ay-mone) and this word literally has two dimensions. First, it is showing mercy and being benevolent. It is forgiving those who are wrong. However, it means so much more. It also means getting right inside the person and feeling, and sympathizing with that individual. It is a deliberate act to fully and completely understand what a person is going through and experiencing.

Whenever I teach or I am asked to describe what mercy is, I often use the other Greek word for mercy. That particular word has the translation and the meaning of stopping or putting an end to one's bending. It's just like the childhood game we use to play in my neighborhood. The game was actually called "mercy." As we played this game, you would face or square off with another person, with both individuals locking their fingers into each other's hands. The object of the game was to bend the opponents fingers as back as you could until someone cried out, "mercy." Literally—this is what being merciful is all about! What this means for a child of God is that when we witness the bending of another person, whether they are bent over because of financial problems and hardships, compounding losses in their lives, experiencing the freshness of bereavement, dealing with the sickness and lingering of a loved one, emotional distress, or whatever the crisis may be, we ought to be moved with compassion to do what we can to stop their bending. At least we ought to be used by God to point them in the right direction. The songwriter of old said, "If I can help somebody along life's way, if I can just help somebody as I travel this way, them my living will not be in vain."

We are called and expected to ease their bending; however, I am afraid that many professed Christians (who are not merciful) are adding to their bending. We have to learn to be compassionate and make some time for people.

Not only are the merciful compassionate, but the other dimension of mercy is that the merciful are forgiving. Some of the most unforgiving people in this world are the people of God. If we really take the time to think about, we probably know of a lot more sinners or unsaved people within the world who forgive quicker, swifter, sooner, faster and better than Christians do with one another. The same people who have had their sins forgiven by God find it difficult to be forgiving one towards another. Many times Christians act just like the unforgiving man in Jesus' parable. However, one man owed and amount too great to repay. The man gave the king a sob story and made a strong appeal for the king to be merciful to him. After the king saw the man's pain and heard his sob story, his heart went out to him and the king erased his debt. But the story goes on that as this same man was leaving the grounds of the palace, he ran into a man who owed him a small amount of money. The forgiven debtor grabbed the man and forcibly choked him while demanding his money. When the man begged for mercy, no mercy was shown. Instead, the one who has just been forgiven of all of his debts by the king had this man (his own debtor) thrown in jail!

Many times we are guilty of treating one another in this same manner. When you take the time and inventory your own shady past, you will realize that God has forgiven us all for so much, yet too many of God's forgiven people are unforgiving towards one another.

Learn how to be forgiving! Jesus did teach us to ask God to help us to be forgiving. In the model prayer, when Jesus teaches His disciples and us how to pray, Jesus said, "When you pray, pray in this manner.....forgive us our debts, as we forgive our debtors."

The Merciful Shall Receive Mercy

The promise that is found and embedded in this Beatitude is that the merciful are shown mercy. In other words, the merciful witness grace. This suggests to me two things I want to share with you. First, we are not going to be perfect. We are not going to live perfect lives. We are not going to act perfectly, or walk and talk perfectly every day in our saved and secured lives. The Apostle Paul picked up this same theme in the book of Romans when he testified and declared, "Every time I would do good, every time I desire to do good, every time I want to do good, evil is always present." Yes, the truth of the matter is that there is a struggle, a war going on in all of our lives. We may have a desire do what is right and pleasing in the eyesight of God, but we are still tempted to do what is wrong. I have already stated that Jesus is teaching us that that the merciful are saved people. However, even saved people will still need to be the benefactors of mercy. Mercy from our fellow man, and mercy from God!

The second thing this theme suggests to me, is something familiar to that old cliché, what goes around, comes around. I briefly shared with you that Jesus taught us a very viable lesson in that model prayer to be forgiving one towards another. But notice something else about the model prayer. Jesus concludes the model prayer with the following words, "For if you forgive men of their trespasses, your heavenly Father will also forgive you. But if you don't forgive men of their trespasses, neither will your Father forgive your trespasses." I don't know about you, but those particular words are more than enough motivation for me to eagerly be ready and willing to forgive somebody else. Reason being, I don't want God withholding His mercy from me!

Let me go back briefly to the parable of the unforgiving servant. Well, when the king heard about what had happened—when he heard how the one he forgave of his debts was so unforgiving and ruthless to his own debtor, the king became very angry. In his anger, the king's spirit of forgiveness had subsided, he turned the once and formerly forgiven debtor over to the jailers to be tortured until he could repay the king every penny of the amount he was due. Can you imagine that? It is hard to believe. But it is possible for someone to actually be forgiven of a debt of millions, and be unable to forgive a debt of hundreds. It is possible for a person to be set free by experiencing God's forgiveness, and then imprison someone else by not forgiving them. When I even think about and deliberate about wanting to wrong somebody who has wronged me, or hold on to a grudge, or to hold on to a heart full of resentment, or just lower the boom on my enemy, I have to take a breath and a step back and just look in the mirror. And as I look in the mirror, I can't help but to see someone who has begged God for His mercy. When I look in the mirror, I see someone who has received so much grace from God. And by my looking in the mirror, it causes me to extend a hand of mercy and grace, even to my enemies.

Let me tell you about a story about a man by the name of Daniel, and his brother, Johnny. Daniel was a big and strong man (he worked out a lot), but yet he had such a tender heart. One day Daniel decided to open his own gym. He went to the bank to apply for a small business loan, but he needed a cosigner. His brother, Johnny, said he would be willing to be a cosigner on the loan. Everything went fine, the rest of the loan process was smooth—and the loan was finally approved. A few days later, Daniel went to the bank to pick up the proceeds from the loan. The bank officer said, your brother was in here earlier. He picked up the money from the loan, and paid off the mortgage on his house. Daniel became very angry. He never thought that his own brother would deceive him. He left the bank and stormed off to his brother's house and knocked on the door. Johnny answered the door, but he had his daughter in his arms—he knew that Daniel wouldn't him if he was holding a child. He was right. Daniel did not hit him, but he did promise that he would break his neck the next time he saw him alone. Daniel had no choice but to open the gym the best way he could and repay the loan. After a while, Daniel started attending a local church. And all heard was the preacher saying, "Forgive us our trespasses, as we forgive those who trespass against us." Every time he went to church, it seems as if Daniel heard nothing from the preacher but, "Do we forgive once, twice or three times? No, we forgive seventy times seven." Daniel kept going to church, and he kept hearing the old preacher say, "If you forgive men of their trespasses, your heavenly Father will forgive you." Through the process of all of those visits, Daniel became a Christian and he started following after the teachings of Christ. However, he still had a problem of letting go of the pain of the past.

One day, Daniel saw his brother. He stepped up to his brother, his fists were clenched, hatred was building and swelling up in his heart, and he grabbed Johnny by the neck. But, he then looked into his brother's face, and his anger began to melt! For as he looked into Johnny's face—he saw the image of their father! As he looked into his brother's facet, he saw the face of their father's. He saw their father's smile. And as Daniel say their father in the face of Johnny, his enemy once again became his brother. Because, it was at that moment that Daniel realized all that his father had done for him! Daniel stopped choking his brother and began to hug him and cry with him.

Before you decide to get even with somebody, before you decide to dig a ditch for somebody who has wronged you, before you decide to remain unforgiving and to act on your rage and resentment, take the time to see the image of our heavenly Father in the face of your enemy! The book of Genesis does declare that we are all made in the image and in the likeness of God.

Look into his or her face, and if you look long enough, you will see the face of the One who showers His grace upon each and every one of us. If you look long enough, you will see the face of the One who has already forgiven you. If you look long enough, you will see the face of the One who gives us new mercies day by day. If you look long enough, you will see the face of the One who loves us unconditionally and who gives us chance, after chance, after chance!

And when you see the face of our Father, you will be able to be merciful, gracious and forgiving—even of your enemy.

Chapter 6
BLESSED ARE THE PURE IN HEART

"Blessed are the pure in heart, for they shall see God" (Matthew 5:8, King James Version).

"Blessed are the pure in heart, for they will see God" (Matthew 58, New International Version).

"God blesses those whose hearts are pure, for they will see God" (Matthew 5:8, The New Living Translation).

"Happy the clean in heart, because they shall see God" (Matthew 5:8, Young's Literal Translation).

When you look at this portion of Jesus' illustrious, illuminating and enlightening Sermon on the Mount, it suggests to us the perplexing yet potential possibility of the fact that one can experience spiritual blindness in this life. You can be around God's word, around God's people, around God's love and God's work and still be blind.

In my periods of meditation on this particular verse, it gave me a new awareness, a new appreciation, and a new understanding for John Newton's hymn, *Amazing Grace*. On John Newton's grave stands a granite tombstone with the following inscription, of which he wrote himself, " John Newton, clerk, once an infidel and Libertine, a servant of slavers in Africa, was by the rich mercy of our Lord and Savior Jesus Christ, preserved, restored, pardoned, and appointed to preach the faith he had long labored to destroy." John Newton was a slave trader. He had for years tried to justify his occupation as a slave trader by misquoting, misunderstanding, and misappropriating what it meant to be a "slave" in the first century Roman Empire and what Paul meant by the phrase, "and slaves obey your master." However, on one of those trips in 1748, it was during a particular stormy voyage when it appeared that he, his ship, his crew, and his cargo would be lost at sea that he came to really know God through Jesus for the very first time—after reading the book *Imitations of Christ*. That is when he was converted and penned those beloved words, "Amazing grace, how sweet the sound that saved a wretch like me. I once was lost, but now I am found. Was blind, but now I see."

I am convinced that there have been and there still are many people who are spiritually blind. It is easy to know of the blindness of those who, for the moment, don't have a desire to be a part of God's family. But, I am primarily referring to those who have been hanging around the fire for a while, those who have been hanging around the church of God for a while, those who have been singing the sweet songs of Zion, those who have been praying seemingly fervent prayers. I am convinced that spiritual blindness is still a problem in our churches.

To illustrate this point, I remember a very heated and passionate conversation I had with another pastor in our community in Nashville, TN. The subject of the issue was a "hot topic" as it relates to church. It was one of those subject matters that causes people to dig their heels in deeply and hold fast to what they believe. However, after we both presented our claims, our arguments backed by Scripture concerning our positions, this pastor came to the point of agreeing with me, but then said, "I am in agreement with you. But, I have held my position for so long, I can't go back and tell my church that I was wrong." This pastor is a living example of so many people today. Even if we are exposed to the light and the truth of God's word, some still purposefully chose to remain in spiritual blindness.

A careful examination of this text suggests that the reason there where those who were spiritual blind, both before and during Jesus' physical, earthly presence and ministry, and the reason there are spiritually blind people even today is because of our unclear, cloudy understanding of what it means to be "pure", and what it means to be "pure in heart."

As Jesus addresses this great multitude, it not only included the twelve disciples he had called to follow Him, but it also included those who were healed of every diseased and sickness through Galilee, and those who were sick and waiting for a healing. But, also included within the confines of this group were the religious leaders of the day—the Pharisees, the scribes, and the Sadducees—those who thought they were pure, those who possessed the wrong idea or concept of religious purity, those who thought they were really seeing God. In this one verse, Jesus challenges their view of God. He challenges their view of religion. He challenges their view of the meaning of the Law. He challenges their interpretation of the purpose of the Law. He challenges their concept of form and formality, rituals and religious order.

I am afraid that many times in our efforts to become so religious, we fallen short in our pursuit of in truly seeing God. Seeing what God desires to do for us. Seeing what God desires to do through us. Seeing what God desires for us to possess and have.

We have become spiritually blind. However, the scales of blindness can be removed from our eyes.

What Purity Is Not

The literal translation for the word "pure" is clean or free from corruption. It gives the idea of no contamination. However, it does not in any way suggest the idea that one is living life free from sin. It does not suggest the idea that one is sinless or that one does not have sinful thoughts or desires. The Apostle John states in I John 1:8, "If we say that we have no sin, we deceive ourselves, and the truth is not in us."

My brothers and sisters, the idea that purity of heart does not mean sinless of life is clear from the inspired record of the history of God's saints—the ones He used in extraordinary ways. Noah became drunk after the flood waters subsided. Abraham lied after beginning his journey of pursuing the promises of God. Moses struck a rock in anger. Job cursed the day of his birth. Peter denied Jesus, not once, but three times. Even Paul, who is the human author and instrument of nearly two-thirds of the New Testament writings, cried out, "O wretched man that I am. Every time I would do good, evil is always present."

As Jesus looked upon the multitude that day, I want to suggest to you that He saw the piousness and the "holier than thou" pretense of the religious leaders and then cried out, "Blessed are the pure in heart." Don't make the same mistake that this group made. They thought their outward acts of cleansing and their outward acts of washing was the answer. The failed to realize just how much they needed the total essence of God in their lives. When God gave the Law to Moses, who was entrusted to give to the people of Israel, Paul reminds us in Romans 3:20 that it was given to provide a standard of righteousness for them to strive to represent God to the pagan nations and communities around them. But, more importantly, it was to point out, identify, and expose Israel's own sin (individually and collectively). Paul declared in that stated passage of Scripture, "The law is the knowledge of sin." In other words, the Law pointed towards just how much we stand in need of God's grace and mercy.

I know that some of you are probably making a self-declaration that you are super saints, that you have already arrived spiritually, that you become untouchable as related to the possibility of succumbing to sin's temptations—but not me. Whenever I read God's word, and whenever I read God's great commandments, I realize that Law of God commands me love God, but grace tells me that God loves me. I realize that the Law commands me to love my neighbor, but grace fills me with God's love for my neighbor. I realize that the Law reveals my sin, but grace revealed Christ to me. I realized that the Law identified and punished every one of my transgressions, but grace pardons each and every one of the acts of my sin. Whenever I read God's word, and whenever I read God's great commandments, I realize that the Law could only condemn me, but the grace of God justifies me freely.

Thank God for His mercy and grace!

So, no, being pure in heart can not mean that we must be perfect, or sin-free or sinless. After all, remember that we are made from the dust of the ground. Our frame is dust, and there is nothing as worthless, as valueless, and as filthy as dust. If we would all be honest, every day we struggle, there is a wrestling match occurring in our lives between doing what is right and wrong in the eyesight of God. No, this phrase does not mean that we are perfect. So, what does it mean?

What Is Purity

In order to answer this question, we have to understand where purity resides. When Jesus speaks or pronounces a blessing upon those who are pure in heart, He is not referring to the organ; but, he uses a word that literally means the seat of the will, mind, intellect and desires of a person. When Jesus said, "Blessed are the pure in heart", He was speaking of the heart as the totality of the inner person. The control power—the cockpit of a person's life. The heart is the origin of our desires. It controls our perceptions, thoughts and affections. The heart is the center of our reasoning, imaginations, and our conscience. It is the seat of our intentions, purpose and will. That is why Solomon was inspired to write in Proverbs 4:3, "Above all else, guard your heart, for it is the wellspring of life."

On one of my first visits to Shreveport, Louisiana, I noticed that there were numerous small oil fields along the way. But, the closer I got to Shreveport, I noticed that there in the distance was a refinery. That was my first time ever seeing a refinery. A refinery is a jungle or a maze of pipes, tanks, tubes, generators, heaters, pumps, filters, valves, hoses, conduits, switches and circuits. However, the purpose of this great maze, the main function of this great jungle of pipes is to live out the meaning of its name. It refines. It purifies. It cleanses oil and gasoline. If you have ever received a bad tank of gas, as evidenced by your car hesitating, sputtering, stalling, clinking and clacking, it will cause you to question the performance quality of that refinery. Well, so it is with us. Evil acts and impure thoughts cause us to question the condition of our hearts.

The heart is the center of the spiritual life. If the fruit of a tree is bad, you don't fix the fruit, you treat the roots of the tree. And if a person's actions are evil, it's not enough to change habits. You have to go a little deeper than that. You have to go to the heart of the problem, which is the problem of the heart.

So the personal question becomes of you, "What is the state of your heart?"

When someone barks at you, do you bark back or bite your tongue? When your schedule is too tight, or your to-do-list is too long, do you lose your cool or do you keep it? When you are offered a little bit of gossip that is marinated in slander, do you turn it down or do you pass it on? When you see the bag lady on the street, do you see her as a nuisance of society or as an opportunity for the glory of God?

The state of your heart determines whether you will hold on to grudges or give grace. The state of your heart will determine whether you drink human misery or taste of God's mercy. And please take heed to Solomon's words of wisdom, "Above all else guard your heart." The reason we have to guard our heart is because no one is exempt from developing a heart problem. Not even David, a man after God's own heart, was exempt. David developed a heart problem when he compiled sin on top of sin, beginning with his affair with another man's wife. However one day, he dealt with his personal problem of the heart as evidenced in his cry of repentance, "Create within me a clean heart....and restore unto me the joy of my salvation."

All of us have had heart problems in the past. How do you know if you have a heart problem? A heart problem occurs if your heart has ever been boastfully proud, and not humble. A heart problem occurs if it has ever been bitter. A heart problem is developing if it has ever been envious or lustful. A problem with heart is occurring if is contrite and is beginning to harden.

But thanks be to the glory of God, your heart can be washed, your heart can be cleansed, and your heart can be made pure.

How do you change the matters of your heart? First, you must have an admission of poverty. God's grace is not received by those who think they have earned it, but only by those who admit they don't deserve it. The second step is the admittance of godly sorrow. Joy only comes to those who are truly sorry for their sins. Sorrow is followed by meekness. The meek are those who are willing to be used by God. Amazed that God would save them, they are just as surprised that God would use them. Next, you start desiring more and more of God. You admit that you are a sinner. You accept Christ as your savior. You confess your weaknesses—and you receive God's strength. You say that you are sorry—and you receive God's forgiveness. And you want more of God—more of His word, more of His ways, and more of His will.

If or since our hearts have been made pure, then there is the promise that we shall see God! You need to understand that you can't see by doing the right things only. You can't see God by saying the right things or by living the right only. There were and are many good morally right people who will not see God, despite all of the outwardly acts of righteousness. Only the pure in heart shall see God.

Only those whose hearts have been washed in the blood of the Lamb (Jesus Christ) will be able to see God!

Oh, I want to see Him, just to look upon His face. There to sing forever of His saving grace. On the streets of glory, just let me lift my voice! Cares all past, home at last, ever to rejoice!

I want to see Him, the One who loves me unconditionally. I want to see Him, the One who cast my sins into the sea of forgiveness. I want to see Him, the One who extend new mercies to me day-by-day and showers His blessings upon me as He passes by my way! I want to see Him, the One who purchased my salvation, bought me my liberty I don't know why He came to love me so—but I want to see the One who looked beyond our faults and saw our needs.

Chapter 7
BLESSED ARE THE PEACEMAKERS

The 9th verse of the 5th chapter of Matthew is probably one of the most misunderstood and poorly interpreted verses of the Bible. As Jesus continues this Sermon on the Mount, he makes the statement, "Blessed are the peacemakers, for they shall called the sons of God." Some have limited the meaning and the application of this verse to mean that Christians should actively be involved in and engaged in such activities where waters are never troubled. Whatever it takes, whatever you have to do to ensure that there is smooth sailing, that is what you do.

However, this is not the correct or proper theological understanding and application of this verse. Let me tell you why I know this not to be the case. First, the word "peace", either in the Hebrew (shalom) or the Greek (eirene) never only means the absence of trouble, but both words always mean everything which makes for a person's highest good. Secondly, Jesus did prepare us for that perplexing promise that we shall have trials and tribulations always. As a matter of fact, in the very next verse, verse 10 of Matthew 5, Jesus is recorded as saying, "Blessed are those who are persecuted because of righteousness sake, for theirs is the kingdom of heaven." There is a deeper meaning to this text than that.

I have stated that the literal meaning of the word peace always means everything which makes for a man's highest good. And what could make for man and woman's highest good than to begin, resume or maintain a right relationship with God!

Mankind had this once.....

When God stood on the threshold of His existence, the Bible declares that He created the heavens and the earth. From the very essence of a spinning mass of nothing, from the very essence of a formless, empty and dark sphere, God's spirit hovered over the waters and called light into existence and separated light from darkness. God then separated water from water with creation of the sky and the atmosphere. God then separated water from water again with the creation of land. He called for the creation of vegetation, seed-bearing plants, trees which bear fruit with sees. He hung the sun to rule by day, placed the moon to rule by night, and hung every star in its own silver socket. God called for the waters, the sky and the land to bring forth every living creature. And then, God made man and woman for the purpose of having fellowship and communion with Him and to be co-laborers and stewards of His creation. Genesis paints such a beautiful picture of peace. Adam and Eve were in perfect fellowship with God, walking with God, talking and communing with God. As a matter of fact, we see the essence of the peace they enjoyed with God in the symbolism in the fact of the Bible stating that they were both naked, and they felt no shame.

Oh.....such purity, such innocence, such a picture of peace is displayed between God and Adam and Eve.

Yes, we had that once, until Adam and Eve gave into the temptation to be like God. Yes, we had such peace, until Adam and Eve yielded to the temptation of sin—and the presence of sin in their lives robbed them and all of mankind of the presence and a righteous standing or relationship with God. The Bible declares that when their eyes were opened, they saw their nakedness and became shameful. When they heard the voice of God walking in the garden, they hid from God because they were shameful.

Every since God banned man from the Garden of Eden, which represented a peaceful state between man and God, He has always reminded man of a promise that would be fulfilled that our restoration was on the way. When Adam and Eve were punished for their sin, God prophesied that there is one who will come and bruise the head of the serpent. Malachi prophesied that Elijah would come before the great day of the Lord. And in the midst of this period from Genesis to Malachi, over a period of 4,000 years—- all of the prophets proclaimed this truth. In Genesis, Christ is seen as the seed of Abraham, through whom we enter into a new family. In Exodus, Christ is seen as manna or the bread from heaven. He is seen as the great High Priest in the book of Leviticus. Joshua pictures Jesus as the Captain of the Lord's host. He is show as the deliverer in the book of Judges. In Ruth, He is seen as our kinsman redeemer. Samuel talks about Him being the seed of David. In the writings of the Kings and Chronicles Christ is seen as King of kings and Lord of lords. Job talks about Christ being our redeemer who lives. Solomon sees Jesus as a friend who will stick closer than a brother, the Rose of Sharon, and the Lilly of the Valley. The prophet Isaiah saw Him as a tried stone, a Wonderful Counselor, a Mighty God, the Prince of Peace, and the offering for our sin. He is Jeremiah's Balm of Gilead. Joel, Amos and Obadiah preached about the coming of Jesus. Jonah proclaimed Him to be risen Savior. Micah, Nahum, Habakkuk, Zephani, Haggai, and Zecharia prophesied about Him. And after the prophet Malachi, there was no word from God. No prophet was called to give or deliver a word of hope. No songs of redemption or deliverance were sung. For approximately 400 years, there was no word from God.

No voice was heard. No vision was seen. Chaos was in the land. Despair was visible, and hope could not be found.

But, in the fullness of time, God sent forth His son as a fulfillment His prophetic word.

As we see Jesus in this text, He has ascended to the mount to preach to his disciples and the crowd. When Jesus sees this crowd, He sees the sin in their lives, He sees how destitute they are, He sees the brokenness and the weariness which is present in their lives. When he sees the multitude, he begins to preach saying, "Blessed are the poor in spirit, for theirs is the kingdom of heaven. Blessed are those who mourn, for they will be comforted. Blessed are the meek, for they will inherit the earth. Blessed are those who hunger and thirst for righteousness, for they shall be filled. Blessed are the merciful, for they shall obtain mercy. Blessed are the pure in heart, for they shall see God. Blessed are the peacemakers, for they shall be called the sons of God." If you look at the progression of this sermon, you see a transition in the life of one who is a sinner, to a saved sinner who is now sanctified and working. After we really look at who we are, really understand the sin problem in our lives, and really mourn over our sin and despise it just as much as God despises it, and after we really see sin the way God sees it and seek to treat it the way God doses, we will move from mourning over our sin to meekly seeking God. And when we seek God and experience God, He gives us His mercy, He gives us a clean heart, and He gives us peace.

Being a peacemaker has got to be more than just putting out fires between man and man here on earth. Being a peacemaker has to do with more than avoiding and steering away from conflicts and troubles. Being a peacemaker has got to be more than walking lightly around certain people in order to avoid arguments and disagreements. In its essence, it is being evangelical! Being a peacemaker means that we all have a responsibility of sharing in this ministry of reconciling broken people into a proper relationship with God through Jesus Christ. We ought to be engaged in winning souls for Christ, sharing the good news of about a risen savior, telling others about the peace we now have and enjoy, telling others about the wonderful change in our lives.

Blessed are the peacemakers! Blessed are the reconcilers!

However, I am afraid, that a good majority of the people of faith and the saved community of Christ is not actively engaged in the work and the ministry of building of lives and winning souls for Jesus, but rather we are more so engaged and active in tearing down.

In the book entitled *Close The Back Door* the thesis or the main idea of this book focuses on the dropouts or the inactive members who unite with the body of Christ. They find a local assembly or congregation they feel comfortable with for their own worship and ministry experiences. But, over a period of time, these same individuals slowly find themselves going out the back door. We must admit that a vast majority of our churches have a problem with these doors.... revolving doors and back doors. Revolving doors constantly find the same people coming in and going out the church. As it relates to back doors, people come in the front door, stay for a little while, and head straight for the back door to never be seen again. In this particular book, the author makes a reference to a Gallup poll. That study or poll provided the following facts: approximately 40% of the American population is unchurched, nearly 90% of the unchurched people were at one time in their life affiliated with some religious community, and over 60% of the unchurched people reported having attended church regularly earlier in their lifetime. This same study suggests that nearly 50% of all Americans have dropped out of active religious participation at some point in their lives. However, 80% returned, but 50% of all Americans have at one point "dropped-out" of church in their lives.

Why do people leave the church? If we are actively engaged as being peacemakers as we are supposed to be, why are people leaving the church?

There is not a reason why people leave, but there are plenty of excuses. Teenagers drop out because of the lust and the temptations offered by the secular world. People move to new communities and never attempt to find a new church home. Illnesses in the family, changes in work schedules, transportation problems, too busy with other interests and the pursuit of personal leisure are all excuses—but there really is no reason.

I contend that people leave the church because of their own personal excuses. However, we cannot deny the fact that sometimes people within the church run people away from the church. Jesus did say, "Blessed are the peacemakers", but every now and then some of us can end up being a troublemaker.

There is a little organ in our mouth which is smaller than the smallest gun, lighter than the lightest fist. Yet, it is just as deadly as a gun and is stronger than any fist. The tongue is less than five inches and it weighs less than 1/8 of a pound. But, it has destroyed many relationships and friendships than can ever be counted. Our tongues have driven many people away from the church. The same tongue which praises God, which gives thanks to God, and which cries out God in prayer has persecuted many Christians, has gossiped about many saints, has killed and assassinated the character and reputation of many Christians. Just read the record. Read what the Bible says about the capabilities of the tongue. Read James 1:26; James 3:6-8; I Peter 3:10; and Psalm 34:13.

The Bible speaks about the improper use of our tongues. David warns us to keep our tongues from evil and our lips from speaking deceit. James warns us by saying, "If any among us think we are religious yet we don't bridle our tongues, our religion is useless." James also that the tongue is a fire, a world of iniquity. Some of the members in the body of Christ, some of the members associated with a local congregation are not as caring, loving, sharing and concerned as they should be. No, but rather we have too many Cain and Abel relationships among the brothers and sisters in the church. Jealous of each other. Envious of one another. Killing each other—maybe not physically, maybe not literally—but killing each other's character.

In Genesis chapter 4, the Bible records the story of Cain and Abel. Cain was a tiller of the ground, Abel was a keeper of sheep. The Bible says they both worshipped God by giving back to Him an offering. In fact, Genesis 4:3 states, "In the process of time, Cain brought an offering of the fruit of the ground to the Lord" But verse 5 say, "Abel brought of the firstborn of his flock." Not a little, not a portion, but the firstborn. Cain gave a portion, but Abel gave all of his increase! And because of this, God had more respect on Abel's offering.

Cain became very angry and killed his own brother. And God asked Cain, "Where is your brother, Abel?" And Cain responded to God with that infamous statement, "I don't know, am I my brother's keeper?"

When I thought about Cain and Abel. When I thought about Cain's statement or question, "Am I my brother's keeper?", I was reminded of a story about an incident which happened in the court system of Massachusetts. There was a man who had been walking on a boat dock, when suddenly he tripped over a rope and fell into the cold, deep water of an ocean bay. He came up sputtering and yelling for help and then he sank again. His friends were too far to get to him. But only a few yards away, on another dock, was a young man sitting in a deck chair. The desperate man shouted, "Help, I can't swim!" The young man, who was an excellent swimmer, only turned his head to watch as the man floundered, panicked and finally drowned. The family of the drowned man was so upset by that display of a lack of care, a lack of concern of the young man that they sued. The court system, however, reluctantly ruled that the young man had no legal responsibility whatsoever to save the other man's life. When I thought about that, the law and the court of Massachusetts agreed with Cain and his presumption, "I am not my brother's keeper."

From the lenses of this story, we see the people of the church today. In looking at these two men, the one who slipped and fell into the bay and the one who sat back and watched the other man drown, I see those among us who are slipping on this journey, with the rest of us, not just sitting back, but watching and gossiping at the same time. Paul told the believers in Christ in the city of Galatia, "Brethren, if a man be overtaken in a fault, you who are spiritual restore such a one in the spirit of meekness" (Galatians 6:1). The word Paul uses for overtaken does not mean a person has committed a deliberate sin. But rather, it is better defined as a slip, as to what might come to a person on an icy road or on a dangerous path. There is another word for sin which deals with deliberate or willful sinning. But this word (paraptoma) means to slip or to be overtaken. Both are sin. Neither is greater or lesser than the other. Sin is sin. But, this word as Paul used in Galatians lets me know that a Christian can be overtaken, taken by surprise, taken unexpectedly, or taken by sin and never suspect it. And when a Christian sees another Christian slipping, the word of God says the real Christian duty or Christ-like thing to do is to help get him or her on their feet again.

The whole atmosphere of the word of God lays the importance not on punishment, but a cure; not on a penalty, but on amendment. But you see, the problem at the church of Galatia and the problem with many Christian churches today is that we are too consumed and busy trying to fit the description and the role, but are too quick to judge the sins of somebody else. And truth be told, the only reason they judge others sins so harshly is because at that moment they had not slipped. We see people slip, we see people being overtaken by sin, we see people being surprised by sin and we want to talk about them.

However, the word of God teaches us not to judge one another, but to restore on another. Paul said, "You who are spiritual restore one another" (Galatians 6:1). He also said, "And all things are of God, who has reconciled us to Himself by Jesus Christ, and has given to us the ministry of reconciliation" (2 Corinthians 5:18). The essences of being a peacemaker is involved in the ministry of reconciliation. The words restore, restoration, reconciliation are all based off the same Greek word which means mending.

In Matthew 4:21, when Jesus was calling his twelve disciples, he called Peter and Andrew while they were fishing and said, "Come, follow me and I will make you fishers of men." He walked a little farther and saw James and John in a boat with their father, Zebedee. They were not fishing. They had been fishing, but now they were mending their nets and Jesus called them. Mending, restoration, reconciliation, are all based from the same Greek word (kattarizo) which means to refit, to repair, to mend that which is broken. James and John were mending their nets, they were repairing their nets, they were fixing their nets, because any fish they would have caught in the net would have fallen out of the net because of the hole. Paul told the church at Corinth, we have this ministry of reconciliation, we have this ministry of mending brokenness.

We have the net ministry....but yet we walk around with broken nets, we walk around with holes in our nets, and we walk around with our nets torn in certain places. The more we talk about individuals, the more we ignore people, the more we criticize people, the more we withdraw from people, shame people, censor and isolate people, spread rumors and slander people the hole in our nets get wider, and wider and wider.

I don't know about you, but the one thing that keeps me from talking about someone when they are down, and the one thing that keeps me from gossiping about someone when they have slipped is that I remember the word of Paul and say to myself, "But by the grace of God, there go I."

If we are going to be peacemakers, we have got to be good stewards over this ministry of reconciliation. God's purpose for sending Christ into the world was to reconcile man back into fellowship with Himself. We all have sinned and come short of the glory of God. Some of you think you are not in sin right now, but let me inform you that your trash stinks too! Sin alienated us from God. Sin destroyed our relationship and fellowship with God.

But when Christ came, loving us despite ourselves and sin, looking beyond our faults and seeing our needs, he met and satisfied all of our needs on Calvary through the shedding of his blood, his death, burial and resurrection. We did not deserve it, but he did it anyway! We are not worthy enough, but he did it anyway! And when he left this earth and went back to his home in glory, Jesus left this ministry of reconciliation, this ministry of restoration, this ministry of mending, he left it in our hands.

And yet, too many of us are guilty of being poor steward of a ministry that was placed in our hands. We are guilt of being poor stewards of a ministry which we have all personally benefited from when our lost souls were saved. We are called to be peacemakers, but too many are busy being troublemakers.

There is a story that is told of this particular family, a rather small family, consisting of only a husband, his wife and their son. Through the years, the father and son's relationship was not the best. As a matter of fact, as soon as the son was able to attend college, the son left home and never returned. He was estranged from his father, but he loved his mother. As the years passed along, the mother and father advanced in years, and the mother's health began to fail. Her doctor had given her pretty grim diagnoses and indicated that she only had a short-while to live. She asked her doctor to do her a favor and contact her son and to tell her son that she wanted to see him just one more time. The doctor granted her wish, contacted her son and said to him, "Your mother is terminally ill. If you would like to see her before she dies, you need to come home soon." The son made his arrangements, caught his flight and made his way home and into the bedroom of his mother. His father was standing on one side of her bed, and he stood on the other side. His mother looked up and smiled at her son. She then turned her head and smiled at her husband. After smiling at them both, she grabbed the hand of her husband with her right hand, and with her left she grabbed the hand of her son. And with the last bit of energy and strength she had, she brought both of their hands together again, and then she died.

Likewise, it was through the death of Jesus on a cross called Calvary that peace was made between God the Father and ourselves. After Jesus ascended back to his home in heaven, this ministry of reconciliation was left within our hands. It is now time for us to extend a hand of peace to those who are living life estranged from the Father's love.

Blessed are the peacemakers.....

Chapter 8
BLESSED ARE THOSE WHO ARE PERSECUTED

Sometimes it gets a little difficult, a little hard to motivate yourself to keep on going, and moving and living after your dreams have turned into a living nightmare. It gets a little difficult to keep on going when your hope has been dashed and when your anticipation has given way to disappointment.

I tell you gets hard!

As we look at the two audiences of our selected text in Matthew 5, we see two audiences who have had their hopes dashed. As Jesus continues his preaching and teaching on the Sermon on the Mount, he is preaching to a crowd (the Jews) who had been waiting for the Messiah to come and deliver them from the persecutions they were facing in their lives. They had been waiting for someone to overthrow their oppressors; and free them from the burden of being under the authority of the Roman Empire. They had been waiting for Messiah to come and validate their God-given status as God's chosen people.

But now, Jesus of Nazareth, the proclaimed Son of God, the promised Messiah, the greater deliver preaches to them and tells them in the sermon that they will still face persecution, not because of them or anything did, but they will face persecution for righteousness sake. Meaning for his sake.

Can't you hear them right now? The writer of the book of Hebrews gives us a vivid description of the persecution the Jewish-Christians were facing in the 10th chapter of Hebrews. Can't you hear them? "We have been on public display as we were being insulted. If it wasn't us, our friends and family were being publicly ridiculed and exposed. Some of us have been locked up in prison and we have lost our material possessions. We are already suffering. We have been waiting on this great deliverer, this great redeemer. We have been waiting on Israel's restoration. But, now you say we have to suffer some more!"

And, some thirty-five years later, after the death, the resurrection and the ascension of Jesus, Matthew was inspired by God to write the gospel of Jesus Christ to a crowd who was on the verge of losing hope. Thirty-five years later, things were not getting better for the Jewish-Christians, if anything it has gotten worse. Palestine, their homeland, has been destroyed again. The temple has been destroyed. Nero was persecuting Christians and feeding them to lions. And as Matthew writes to the people of Israel and the Jewish-Christians, he is inspired by God to write as he remembers Jesus from the mountainside on day and said, "Blessed are those who are persecuted for righteousness sake, for theirs is the kingdom of heaven."

One of the hardest questions a child of God has to wrestle with is, "Why must the righteous suffer?"

I have been there myself. In the first year of my pastorate, almost seventeen years ago, the Lord allowed me to experience a blessing and a burden, both of which were tied to the same person within the same year. As a pastor, you never forget the first person you baptize, and you never forget your first funeral. I had the privilege of baptizing a little girl named Stephanie when she was about eight or nine years old. She was a beautiful and a sweet little girl. During the course of that same year, when our state convention was in session, I received a disturbing call that informed me that Stephanie had drowned while swimming in a nearby lake. I had to ask the question of the Lord that day, "Why must the righteous suffer?"

There are many times when the faithful suffer the consequences of the faithless. Anytime a person takes a step in the right direction, only to have his feet knocked out from under him; anytime a person does a good deed, but suffers evil results; anytime a person takes a stand, only to land flat on his face the question will begin to fall like rain. "If God is so good, why do I hurt so bad? If God is really there, why am I here? What did I do to deserve this? Did God slip up this time? Why are the righteous persecuted?"

Yes, the questions just fall like rain whenever the faithful experience the consequences of the faithless.

In his book, *Disappointment with God*, Philip Yancey quotes a letter that articulates the problem of unmet expectations in all its excruciating reality. Meg Woodson lost two children to cystic fibrosis, and her daughter's death at age twenty-three was particularly traumatic. The following words speak of her pain and doubt as she struggled to cope with what happened.

She said, "I was sitting beside her bed a few days before her death, when suddenly she began screaming. I will never forget those shrill, piercing, primal screams...It's against this background of human beings falling apart...that God who could have helped, looked down on a young woman devoted to Him, quite willing to die for Him, to give Him glory, and God decided to sit on His hands and let her death top the horror charts for cystic fibrosis deaths."

So the question is, does God sometimes sit on His hands? Does God sometimes choose to do nothing when He has the power to do everything? Does God sometimes decide to be silent, even when I am screaming at my loudest?

God wants us to be proclaimers of His word. God wants us to be doers of His word, fruit-bearing branches, disciples of Christ, lights to a dark world, and salt to a flavorless society. But sometimes, when troubles come in our lives...sometimes when sickness runs rampant in our bodies...sometimes when persecutions comes our way... sometimes when the storm begins to brew and the winds become contrary...sometimes...sometimes it does seem like God is sitting on His hands.

What do you do when God sits on His hands?

When it seems like God is silent during your most troubling moments, I want to suggest to you to remember three very important things, but I want you to share this with you from Revelations 2:8-10. "And to the angel of the church in Smyrna write: The first and the last, who was dead, and has come to life, says this: "I know your tribulation and your poverty (but you are rich), and the blasphemy by those who say they are Jews and are not, but are a synagogue of Satan. Do not fear what you are about to suffer. Behold the devil is about to cast some of you in prison, so that you will be tested, and you will have tribulation for ten days. Be faithful until death, and I will give you a crown of life.""

The Divine Presence Of God

Of the seven churches of Asia Minor, only two received no words of condemnation from our Lord and Savior—and one of those two churches was the church at Smyrna. No blame, no word of rebuke, not one word of chastisement is given to this church.

Although there was no room for correction, or chastisement, or condemnation, the church was still not without its problems. The church at Smyrna still had to face the persecutions, the challenges and the troubles of this world. The believers at Smyrna had been through a lot—they had to suffer physical persecution, lost their possessions and their wealth, and their names were being slandered and scandalized.

But to top all of this off, Jesus basically says, "I know it is dark now, but it is going to get darker before the new day breaks. I know it is bad now, but it is going to get worse before it gets better. I know you are crying now, but you have to shed more tears before a smile comes across your face. I know you are hurting now, but you must hurt some more before the hurt goes away. I know your works, your tribulations, your poverty, the blasphemy of them who speak against you. Fear none of those things which you shall suffer. Behold the devil will cast some of you into prison that you may be tried and you shall have tribulation."

As believers, our road has not always been easy. Our nights have seemingly outnumbered our days. Our bad days have seemingly outweighed our good days. As believers we have shed many tears, the going has been tough, the road has been rough, and the hills have been hard to climb. And yet, our Savior says it is going to get worse before it gets better. But even in the promise of more bad news, Jesus is reminding us that His presence is near. He said, "I am the First and the Last." In this statement, Jesus is reminding us that He has knowledge about us, He knows what we been through, and He knows what we will go through. Also, His words remind us that He will comfort and strengthen the faithful and give ease to our troubled minds.

"I am the First..."

Can't you hear Him right now? "I am at the head and beginning of all things. All were ordered and arranged according to the counsel of my will."

"I am the Last..."

Scripture reminds us that when men and Satan have done their all and nothing is left more for them to do, and they have gone to their own places, Jesus will remain. And in His kingdom there shall be no end. In other words, since Jesus is there in the beginning and His promise is given that He will be there in the end, He is letting us know that He will be there in between.

You ought to be glad that Jesus is present. Because Jesus was present, blind Bartimaeus eyes were opened, Jairus' daughter was resurrected, Peter's mother-in-law was healed of her fever, 5000 men plus women and children were fed by two fish and fiver barley loaves of bread, and woman with an issue of blood for twelve long years was healed of her hemorrhaging disease. Whenever Jesus shows up, He will show out! He will shut the lion's mouths, take the heat out of the flame, calm raging seas, and raise bowed-down heads. He did promise that He would never leave us or forsake us.

This entire discussion on First-Last reminds me that the battle has already been fought and the victory has already been won.

The Promise Of Power Found In His Resurrection

"....which was dead and is alive."

Jesus continues to give divine support for an afflicted people by reminding them of Calvary. We can make it when things get worse before they get better because we know for a fact that Jesus made it even in the worse of circumstances. Of His own free will, he went down into the pains and the darkness of death on a hill called Calvary.

When I look at the conquest of a shameful death at Calvary, it helps me to make it through the darkest moments of my life. We have to remember that Jesus knows how we feel. He was tried and tested, and endured the hardships of tribulations. He knows all about what we go through. He knows all about how we feel. He entered into death so that He might be better able to help us, aide us, and assist us. Sin and hell did their worst against Him; but yet, Jesus cries out, "I live forever more."

Paul reminds us in the book of Corinthians to always look towards the empty tomb whenever you feel like giving up, giving in, or the nights appear to get longer and longer, or the burdens get too heavy to carry. Look towards the empty tomb! Paul says look to the empty tomb and remember you have the victory. He said, "O death, where is your sting? O grave, where is your victory? The sting of death is sin, and the strength of sin is the law. But thanks be to God who gives us the victory through our Lord Jesus Christ."

I want to suggest to you that you can run on just a little bit farther, because you know that our Savior lives.

The Promise Of Divine Limitations

Jesus said, "Fear none of those things which you shall suffer; behold the devil will cast some of you into prison, that you may be tried; and you will have tribulations ten days."

I like that I tell you! God will not let His children suffer for too long. God will not put any more on us than we can bear. The phrase in this text suggests the idea that "ten days" is symbolic that troubled days will end. "Ten days" is symbolic that crying days will cease. "Ten days" is symbolic that nights will give way to the break of a new day. "Ten days" is symbolic that sorrows will give way to joy. "Ten days" is symbolic that bad days will give way to good days.

So, fear not! It may be dark now, but there is a bright side somewhere. Fear not! Weeping may endure for a night, but hold on to the promise that joy is coming in the morning.

Chapter 9
So, What Does It Really Mean To Be Blessed By God?

So, what is a blessing?

I think sometimes we get blessings mixed up with other things, like presents. You can go to a store and buy a present, but you can't go to a store and buy a blessing from God. God gives you a talent when you are born. Sometimes you are born with an innate ability for athleticism or for music. But a blessing is even more than that. A blessing comes from the sovereign God who gives undeservedly to whom He wants, whenever He wants, however He wants.

When we hear or think of the words "bless, blessed or blessing"—in its essence it is just too broad for us to fully understand. Biblically—there are seven prominent Hebrew and Greek words as it relates to the word "blessed." I just one to share with you just two of those words (one Hebrew and one Greek)—the ones that are used the most in the Old and New Testaments.

In the Old Testament, the word barak is used approximately three hundred and two (302) times. There are two meanings for this word. The word barak is used biblically when mankind would bless God—by kneeling in His presence or by using words of praise or adoration to God. It means to bless God as an act of adoration or praise. But, when you read the Scriptures carefully, this same word is used for God blessing man and woman. We know God does not pay homage or worship to man. The creator does not bow, kneel, praise or worship the creation, but rather when this word is used of God blessing man, it is used as God blessing man as a benefit.

I like that word benefit........it literally means a GIFT. As a gift made to help someone! It literally means something that is good..... something that is advantageous!

In the New Testament, there are two words I want to lift up and those words are eulogeo and makarios. Eulogeo literally means to speak well of.......we praise God.....we adore God...we speak well of God for who He is and for what He has done! Makarios literally means fortunate or well-off. Here it is—we are fortunate or well-off not because of what we have, but because of who has us. We are the blessed one or BLESSED. We possess the favor of God. In essence, it is that state of the mark of the fullness from God. It indicates the state of the believer in Christ. It's all spiritual.

Jesus is the master teacher on prosperity. This claim is evidenced by his sermons as recorded in the fifth and sixth chapters of the Gospel according to Matthew. Throughout the course of this book, we have been on a journey through the fifth chapter, but there is something I have intentionally not shared with you until. Every time you see the word blessed in Matthew 5, Jesus is using the Greek word "makarios". Remember, this word gives the idea of one being well-off or fortunate because of the spiritual blessings received from God. But, when you read Matthew 6:33, "But seek first His kingdom and His righteousness, and all these things will be added to you", the word of God promises that other things (physical, fiscal, and monetary things) will be added to us after we have realized the spiritual blessings we have. However, the problem for the majority of people is that we seek OTHER THINGS first......and seek SPIRITUAL blessings last. And it won't work that way. If it does, it is only going to be temporary. The teachings of Christ on prosperity and blessings is that He prioritizes a right relationship with God first, before reaping what we deem to be "prosperous" things.

Obedience Is A Key

To be blessed by God is based on the biblical truth that God promised to bless His obedient children. But, I won't you to know that the operative word here is "obedient." It is a fact that God loves us unconditionally, but most of His promises of blessings come with a condition. There is some fine print in God's contracts. In secular contracts, often the fine print is deceptively positioned and located in hidden places. Sometimes you have to get a magnifying glass to read the fine print. Sometimes you have to do like Fred Sanford—and pull at four and five different pairs of glasses to read the fine print in a secular contract. But, unlike secular contracts, God does not hide the fine print, we just choose to ignore it!

Do you want to know what our problem is? We want the blessings without the conditions. We want the crown without the cross. We want the joy of the resurrection without the suffering of the crucifixion. We want Easter Sunday without Good Friday. Obedience is a major key. There is no denying the fact that bible contains many promises from God that He wants His children to prosper in this life. However, the conditions to many of these promises is general found in the fine print of obedience and total dependence on Him, especially through the temporary circumstances and conditions of life.

It should be worth noting, despite what some people teach and preach—God has not cursed people who are poor in material wealth. As a matter of truth, biblically speaking, God has always found special favor with the oppressed, the least and the unlikely. From this truth, we get a biblical, theological foundation for a liberation gospel. We must remember, the result of liberation is freedom. Freedom for what? Freedom to be all that God would have us to be. Freedom to prosper spiritually and materially. Resurrections do follow crucifixions. Joy does come in the morning. There is a crown after the cross. There is a bright side somewhere, and there is a blessing on the other side of through. The sad reality is that many times believers do not demonstrate a total dependence on God as they journey through the temporary, negative circumstances of life. If that is where you are in your journey with God, I want to help you to receive the blessings on the other side of through without ignoring the "through." So many times we often hear that pitiful cry resonating from the lips of the believer, "I am going through." This is what it is—a pitiful cry and not a testimony. It does not become a testimony until you come out on the other side of through. Remember David in Psalm 23? He was walking through the valley of the shadows of death, but once he made it though noticed the blessings he received. He realized the Lord's presence in his life. He realized the Lord's protection over his life. He realized the Lord's preparations for his life. He realized the Lord's power during his life. And he realized the Lord's pouring-out upon his life. Yes, there is a blessing on the other side of through.

Asking—A Key Factor To Being Blessed

"...We have not because we ask not" (James 4:2—KJV).

Hide this scripture in your heart, make it a part of your constant thinking and you will be blessed. Asking is the most simple and obvious, yet the most underused, ignored, and neglected factor in being blessed. Why? Because we have not yet fully internalized that it is the nature of God to bless, and we cannot spiritualize in our understanding the unlimited wealth of God. We cannot conceive that we have a generous, extravagant Father with unlimited blessings. We seem to think that because He has blessed us once, and He blessed our friends and relatives, that He must be running short or running out of blessings.

God's blessings are unlimited. If we keep on asking over and over again, then He will keep on blessing over and over again. We seem to think that we worry God when we keep asking and that because He blessed us once, He does not want to hear from us again.

Also, we are so pious in our praying that we feel we are selfish if we keep asking God continuously for blessings. God is like any loving parent who wants his children to have all that He has for them and who enjoys the relationship that takes place in the asking. Matthew 7:7-11 gives us some insight into God's parenting nature.

"Ask, and it will be given you; seek, and you will find; knock and it will be opened to you. For everyone who asks receives, and he who seeks finds, and to him who knocks it will be opened. Or what man is there among you who, when his son asks for a loaf, will give him a stone? Or if he asks for a fish, he will not give him a snake, will he? If you then, being evil, know how to give good gifts to your children, how much more will your Father who is in heaven give what is good to those who ask Him!"

Jesus admonishes us over and over again to ask! Notice, the conditions of abiding and asking in His name.

"Whatever you ask in My name, that will I do, so that the Father may be glorified in the Son. If you ask Me anything in My name, I will do it." (John 14:13-14).

"If ye abide in Me, and My words abide in you, ask whatever you wish, and it will be done for you." (John 15:7).

I believe that God would not repeatedly tell us to ask if He did not want us to ask repeatedly. We shouldn't hesitate to make asking a constant point in our prayers. We should ask God over and over again to bless us. How would we feel if when we get to heaven and Peter, the keeper of the gate, took us on a tour and showed us all of the unclaimed blessings, including the ones that had our names on them? There are many blessings that don't get claimed because we simply fail to ask. How many times have we been blessed with blessings for which we did not ask? Well, they are only a fraction of the blessings that have our names on them; we must ask for the others. Remember, one of the key factors in being blessed is knowing who we want to become in Christ and having the courage to ask for it.

Living The Blessed Life Means Listening To The Voice of God

God has promised that if we would listen diligently, He will bless us in powerful ways. God wants us to hear Him and He desires for us to do His will. God is a promise-keeper, and He has signed a contract to bless us. However, a word of caution is needed. We must not forget to read the fine print. Hearing must also be followed by doing. The word "hear" in the Bible means "to do." Hearing means doing. Hearkening or listening to His voice means keeping His commandments.

The blessings of God are not automatically poured out upon people. God is not a robot, not a mechanical being that acts impulsively or on the spur of the moment without thought or purpose. The blessings of God are not the result of a reflex emotion that arouses God to bless this and that person. The blessings of God are not poured out indiscriminately, at random, in a chaotic manner. God demands something of a person before He blesses that person. God's blessings are conditional. A person has to do something in order to receive God's blessings.

If we hearken to His voice, we will be blessed.

Old Testament Lesson—Deuteronomy 28:1-14

The Old Testament scripture reference is from the book of Deuteronomy and is called the Second Law. It was written by Moses. This book was written after the exodus experience, but before the Promised Land experience. This text was written after the Red Sea experience, but before the crossing of the Jordan River experience. God had led His people out of bondage in Egypt—but Egypt was still in them!

The children of Israel were camped in the plains of Moab close by the river Jordan, right across from the great city of Jericho. They were poised to cross the river and enter the promised land. But before they entered, Moses felt the need to preach a series of messages to the people. He needed to make sure that the people understood exactly how they were to live in the promised land of God.

In essence, Deuteronomy is the preaching of Moses during the days when the Israelites were camped beside the Jordan River, preparing themselves to enter the promised land. At this point, the messages are nearing completion. Moses has almost accomplished his purpose. The people are prepared, as much as Moses is capable of preparing them. Only one more thing remains: the people needed to renew their covenant with God. They needed to make a rededication, a recommitment to God, before actually entering the promised land. The present passage deals with the blessings and cursings of the covenant. The people were to be blessed if they obeyed God, but cursed if they disobeyed Him.

Moses had guided God's people for nearly forty years. Now Moses is of some age and God says to him, give them the Law one more time. So, old man Moses stands up and says one more time, "I want to tell you it shall come to pass that if thou shall hearken diligently unto the voice of God and observe all these commandments, God will bless you. He will bless your coming in and your going out. He will bless you so you won't ever be the tail, you will always be the head. He will bless you so that blessings will even overtake you. God says if you hearken diligently, I will bless you in a very, very special way."

Let us examine this covenant, promissory contract. Anytime anybody gives us a contract we should to read it carefully. As we read this covenant, promissory contract carefully, let us make sure we read the fine print.

God Can Bless Anywhere

First, look at what God says in verse 3. He says that I will bless you wherever you are. I will bless you in the city, and I will bless you in the field. God can bless you wherever your place is. And somebody needs to know that your current location will not restrict your blessings from God. Geography doesn't matter and is not a prerequisite for God's blessings. He can bless you on the job or in school. He can bless you walking down the street or riding in a car or on a bicycle. He can bless you in your church or any other church.

I know what people say—but we do not have to be in a certain church to be blessed. People even mistakenly name their churches as the source of their blessings. We do not have to be under a certain pastor to be blessed. God is the Blesser. He can bless any church, anywhere. He will bless a church in the suburbs or in the country. We can be blessed in the inner city or on the farm. We can be blessed in the field or on any continent, or in any country. God is a blessing God and He says that we do not have to be in a certain place to be blessed. He will bless us where we are. Make sure you are in your place, whether it's downtown or uptown or midtown.

God Will Bless Our Efforts

God will also bless whatever we produce. He will bless the fruit of our body. He will bless our children. He will bless our cattle. He will bless our work. In other words, He will bless the work of our hands. He will bless our endeavors.

He will give an increase to our product or our production. Keep on sowing seeds, He says, and He will give the increase.

In other words, keep on working on that project, even though it seems like the boss does not care. It may seem like the boss doesn't really care. We may not get a feather in our cap. We may not get a bonus or a raise, but God says keep on working on that project and He will give the increase.

We must keep on praying for the unsaved persons in our families. It may look like things are down and that they will never hearken to God's Word, but if we keep on praying for them, He will give the increase. God will bless.

We must keep on witnessing to that wayward, too-hot-to-trot daughter. It may seem like there isn't any hope, but God will bless. We must keep on praying in faith for that prodigal son that has dropped out of school. God will give the increase. We must keep on praying for that spouse that is strung out on drugs. God has promised us in a promissory contract that He will bless us. But we had better be careful and read the fine print.

God Will Bless Our Necessities

If the people obeyed God...their population would grow, over-flow with fruitfulness; their livestock would grow and increase; their crops would grow and increase; their daily food would always be pro-vided. The point is striking: the people of God would always have an abundance of everything. Everything they owned would be fruit-ful and increase in value. They would grow as a people and as a na-tion. Moreover, their livestock would increase more and more, and their crops would produce an abundant harvest. They would develop a strong economy, be financially secure. And note the blessing of daily food: the very basic necessities of human life—food and water—would always be provided for them.

That is why we can sing with conviction the words of the hymn—Great is Thy Faithfulness. Morning by Morning new mer-cies I see! ALL I have needed Thy hands have provided. Great is Thy faithfulness, Lord unto ME!

God Will Bless Our Coming and Going

Then God says, in verse 6, if we hearken diligently, He will bless our coming in and our going out. In other words, when we leave home, we will know everything will be all right when we get back home. If we hearken diligently, we won't have to worry about Jody and Ray Ray coming to our house. When we go out, we won't have to worry about who else is coming in, and when we come in, we don't have to worry about who is going out the back door. God will bless our coming in and our going out.

The blessing of all daily activities is promised to the obedient person. No matter where a person is—coming into or going out of the home—God will bless him. The only condition is obedience. If the person is walking with God, following God with all his heart, then God blesses him. Where the believer is, at home or away, does not matter. What matters is obedience. If the believer is walking after God, obeying Him, then God blesses his daily activities—all of them.

God Will Bless Us With Victory

In verse 7 God says, hearken to the Lord and the Lord will smite our enemies. The blessing of victory over all enemies is promised to the obedient person. Protection or security is a most wonderful promise given by God to the believer. The enemy will come in one way and go out seven ways. Do we hear what the Lord is saying? First of all, He is going to take care of our enemies. They will be smitten.

Note exactly what is said to the Israelites about this wonderful promise: if an enemy rises up against you, that enemy will be defeated before your very presence. No matter who the enemy is nor how strong and numerous, the enemy will be defeated. Note the graphic description: the enemy will come at you from one direction, but he will flee from you in seven directions, flee as a defeated, scattered foe.

The enemies who confronted the Israelites were a symbol of the spiritual enemies that confront the believer. As the believer marches to the promised land of heaven, enemy after enemy confronts him, enemies such as...backbiters, despisers, stormy trials, financial difficulties, loss of job, and doubt and unbelief. The enemies that attempt to overthrow and conquer the believer are innumerable. But the promise of God is strong: if the believer will obey God, keep His holy commandments, God will give him victory over the enemies that oppose him. Victory is assured, assured if the believer will just obey God.

Our enemies will come in over here (one way), and when God gets through with them, they will go out over there, there, there, there, there, there, and there (seven ways). Our enemies will come in one door, and God will run them out seven different doors. God will bless us by continually kicking the devil's tail.

Reading the Fine Print

God has blessed us. He is a promise-keeper, and He has given us a contract. But we need to read the fine print. There is some fine print in every contract. Usually it is preceded by some little subjunctive clause or something that says "if." When we read a contract, we should read it and look for "buts" and "ifs." God also has some "ifs," so we need to read the fine print.

It bothers me when I hear folks on TV talking about "name it and claim it," believing that we can speak something into existence. No! No! No! The blessings in this passage don't even REMOTELY resemble that—because they are conditional.

However—there is such a thing as "self-talk." The Bible says— sometimes you have to encourage yourself! David, one day encouraged himself in the Lord. He gave himself a good "self-talk." I play a little golf—and when I play, I talk to myself. When I get behind or hit a bad ball, I say, "Come on Clint." When I hit a hook or a slice I say, "Straighten it out Clint—straighten it out." When I hit the ground behind my ball—and the ball doesn't go anywhere, I say, "Keep your head down, Clint." I was talking to myself. "Clint you can do it. You've got to win this one." I was talking to myself and it was helping me to win the game. And so it is with our strive to be obedient to God, you have to learn how to talk to yourself.....encourage yourself to do what God desires for you to do.

Read the fine print. I see some of those little "ifs" in here. In verse 2 you find, "And all these blessings shall come on thee and overtake thee, if..." In verse 9, "the Lord shall establish thee an holy people unto himself, as he hath sworn unto thee, if..." Our problem is that we are not reading the fine print. We want the blessing, but we don't want to obey the fine print.

God has signed a contract with us. He is a promise-keeper. We need to get away from this prosperity gospel that puts us under the false illusion that we have the power to speak a blessing into existence. What about the people suffering through floods and other natural tragedies? Do we think that God has forsaken them for some reason or another? We need to understand that God is God, and God is God all by Himself, and God will always be God.

If we hearken unto Him, we will never be the tail. In verse 12, the scripture says that we won't be the borrowers, we will be the lenders. Hear what God is saying. He says, we won't be the receivers, we will be the givers. Indeed, it is better to give than to receive. I can't understand why people pray only to receive stuff. I don't want to just receive, but I want to just give. I don't think we have thought this through. We should want to be the givers also. But we pray to receive—let me receive this and that, and some money. However, I am now praying to give some money. We need to check ourselves out. It is more blessed to give than to receive.

Needs vs. Wants

The Bible says that God will supply all of our needs according to His riches in glory (Philippians 4:19). He is a good supplier. He will supply our needs, not our wants. As a matter of fact, the Bible tells us that the Lord is our Shepherd, we shall not want. The reason why we have not been blessed is that we have been dealing too much in the wanting business and too little with our need business.

God says He will supply all of our needs according to His riches in glory. Do we know that our Father is rich? Do we know that we are joint heirs to the throne with Jesus? Do we know that everything that Jesus owns, we own? Do we know that Jesus is not just our Savior, but He is our elder brother? Do we know that our Father owns all the cattle on the hills? Do we know that the earth is His and the fullness thereof? And He says He will supply ALL of our needs.

Blessings that Follow Us And Blessings That Go Before Us

I like what verses 1 and 2 say...if you hearken diligently, blessings will overtake you. In another section, I will talk about blessings following us. In other words, wherever we go, surely goodness and mercy will follow us all the days of our life.

God has some other blessings. Goodness and mercy have our backs, but God has blessings that will overtake us. Do we know what that means? It means that there are going to be some blessings that will run ahead of us. So not only do we have blessings behind us, but some blessings are going to run in front of us. This means that everywhere we go we will be bumping into blessings. When we turn this way, we bump into blessings. When we go another way, we bump into some more blessings. When we go yet another way, we bump into some grace. When we go over here, we bump into some goodness. When we go over there, we bump into some love. Mercy back there, grace up here...God is a promise-keeper, if we hearken diligently. If we hearken diligently, He will bless us.

Chapter 10
Being Blessed By God—Also Means Being Blessed Through Faith

We all want to be blessed. Here is good news for us today: we can be blessed. I can guarantee it because I know the key that unlocks the door to blessing. The key is faith. Faith is the key that unlocks the door of blessing.

Two simple propositions undergird God's promise of blessing. One is that God promises blessings to those who have faith. Second, it is impossible to please God without faith. Therefore, faith lets us please God and be blessed. Faith pleases God and faith blesses us. Notice there is a promise that if we please God, He will bless us. Faith is the key that unlocks the blessing door.

FAITH—- Forsaking All I Trust Him!

One reason many of us are not blessed in the manner that God has purposed and designed for our lives—may be because our trust is anchored in everything else but Him (GOD).

A Biblical Example

Our Old Testament text from Genesis, the first book of the Bible, is a very pivotal point in all Christianity; it is where God called out Abraham to look for a city. (Genesis 12: 1-3).

The blessings that are available to us today began with the promises God made to Abraham, the father of faith. Look at Abraham. God called Abraham to go and look for a city—to go to a foreign country. He was called to go, not knowing where he was going. He was called to go, not knowing whom he would meet when he reached his destination. He was called to go, not knowing where he would eat or where he would sleep or where he would live. He was just called to go. Sometimes God asks you just to step out on faith. God says go, so all you need to do is just go.

Abraham's experience illustrates the biblical definition of faith. The writer of Hebrews says, "Now faith is the substance of things hoped for, the evidence of things not seen" (Heb. 11:1). In other words, something that is evident yet we have not seen it. If we can see something, we can't call it faith. If we can reason it, we can't call it faith. If we can put it into a framework of deductive reasoning or inductive reasoning and have a rational predictable outcome, then we cannot call it faith. Remember, we walk by FAITH and not by SIGHT!

Look at this text.....it's more than just the command "go" that is being implied. But, if you are going to be blessed by God, it is also a call of separation. Therein lies another problem or hindrance to the blessings of God being realized in our lives. Many of us are attempting to "go" or follow after God, but we are taking the lust and the love of the world with us. There was the call of God to Abram, the call to live a life of separation. God called Abram to the most difficult task a person can ever face: that of changing his life, of completely turning around and forsaking everything in this world he loves and finds dear. God called Abram to leave and forever separate himself from... his country, his relatives, his father's house, the family's possessions and property, the love, care, support, security, and approval of the people he knew and held dear.

Why? Why would God call Abram to give up the very things that mean so much to a person? For this very reason: the people and things of the world apparently meant too much to Abram. Abram was putting his world and family before God, putting their love, security, possessions and approval before God.

How do I know this? Because this was God's second call to Abram. He had not followed through with God's first call. Remember, Abram and his family were now living in Haran. They had left Ur of the Chaldeans some years before when God first called Abram (Genesis 11:31-32). God's first call issued at Ur is unquestionable. Scripture is clear about this. Stephen, in his great sermon right before his martyrdom, declared that God first called Abram in Ur: "And he said, Hear me, brethren and fathers! The God of glory appeared to our father Abraham when he was in Mesopotamia, before he lived in Haran, and said to him, Leave your country and your relatives, and come into the land that I will show you" (Acts 7:2-3). God Himself reminded Abram of the first call: "And he [the Lord] said unto him, I am the LORD who brought you out of Ur of the Chaldeans, to give you this land to possess it" (Genesis 15:7). Nehemiah referred to the first call: "You are the Lord God, Who chose Abram and brought him out from Ur of the Chaldees, and gave him the name Abraham" (Neh. 9:7). The first call was not to Terah (Abraham's father)—but to Abraham in the land of Ur! The second call is now issued while Abram is in Haran.

The point is this: apparently Abram did not go all the way with God, not when God first called him. Abram started out following the promises of God when he left Ur to begin his journey, but he stopped in Haran, far short of the promised land. Truth of the matter is that many of us haven't realized the promise of blessings in our lives—because we got stuck in Haran! We got sidetracked in Haran! We became too comfortable living in Haran! But thank God for a second call! Thank God for another opportunity to hear his voice again! Thank God for another chance!

But, the question becomes, "Why?" Why a second call? Was his reason legitimate, or was he distracted by some worldly attraction or greed? Abram's reason for stopping in Haran is not stated;

therefore, we cannot be absolutely sure why he remained in Haran. But we can say is that Abraham got distracted in Haran. But based upon the threefold demand of God for separation, the weight seems to be that Abram had backslid, that he had lost sight of God's call to separation. God was apparently striking at the very things that had distracted Abram from God's call, striking at the very things that had led Abram to backslide and forsake the promised land.

In our personal lives we have to step out on faith. Too many of us are holding on to the trunk of the tree. Faith is out on the limb. We have to turn loose of the trunk and go out on that limb. Faith is the evidence of things unseen.

The question that we have to raise is, "How do we have evidence of what we cannot see?" We have to raise that question to God and in light of Scripture. The Bible tells us that faith is not as blind as we often think. Faith is blind, yet faith can see. How? Faith is the evidence of things unseen, which means faith is blind, yet faith can see. The answer is that God never asked us just to have faith. God asked us to have faith in Him.

God's Promise to Abraham and Us

Look what God promised Abraham in our Scripture text. First, He promised Abraham that He would make him a great nation. God told Abraham when he started out, not knowing where he was going, He would bless him and make his name great. Second, God promised to make Abraham a blessing. In other words God is saying, "Not only will you be blessed, but I'm going to make you a blessing." Then He promised, "I will bless the ones that bless you, and I will curse the ones that curse you."

God says to Abraham, "I will bless all your seed." Isn't that wonderful that He said He would bless all of Abraham's seed? Abraham is the father of faith. We are all of the seed of Abraham. All these blessings that Scripture mentions are available to Abraham's seed. That means us. Romans 4:16 (KJV) says, "Therefore, it is of faith, that it might be by grace; to the end the promises might be sure to all the seed; not to that only which is of the law, but to that also which is of the faith of Abraham; who is the father of us all."

God says that I can be in the blessing channel. By faith, God has promised to make us a blessing. By faith, God has promised to bless us. By faith, God has promised to bless others who bless us and to curse others who curse us (He will do the reaping!)

What then is our problem? Our problem is that we are too stressed to be blessed. Conversely, Dr. Suzan Johnson-Cook titled her book Too Blessed to Be Stressed. Our problem is just the opposite. We are too stressed to be blessed. We are too stressed out on loving the blessing and not loving the One who blesses. We love what God can bless us with, but we aren't loving God. We are too stressed out on self to be blessed by God. God will not bless a lover of self and things. Our problem is that we have our eyes on the blessing, and we need to have our eyes on the Blesser. God will not bless a lover of houses and of cars. God will not bless a lover of clothes and of money. God blesses those who bless Him. We have our eyes on blessings when we should have our eyes on the Blesser.

Faith And Blessings—Romans 4:13-16

I want to share with you three things concerning faith that ties into blessings. First, faith blesses us with righteousness: "Now the Lord said to Abram, Go forth from your country and from your relatives and from your father's house, to the land which I will show you" (Genesis 12:1) Romans 4:13 ays, "For the promise to Abraham or to his descendants that he would be heir of the world was not through the Law, but through the righteousness of faith."

We should be concerned with the righteousness of faith. God takes our faith and makes our wrongs right. That's what the Bible says. How else can we be righteous? All of us are wrong. If we think we're right, we're wrong. We may have been reading psychology books that say, "I'm okay, you're okay." We're not okay. Read the Bible. All have sinned and fallen short of the glory of God. All of us. Can we find a righteous man? No, not one. Romans 4:25 says, "He who was delivered over because of our transgressions, and was raised because of our justification." By the resurrection of Jesus, we are justified.

What does it mean to be justified? It means to be made right with God. That's why the song says, "In His righteousness I stand complete." God takes our faith and turns our incompleteness into something complete. God takes our faith and turns our wrong into right. God takes our unholiness and changes it into holiness. God takes our imperfections and turns them into perfections. How else do we dare stand in a sanctuary in the presence of God and say we are raising holy hands? We dare to do so because God takes our faith and makes unholy hands holy. God, by faith, justifies us.

It's a blessing to be justified. Faith blesses us with justification and righteousness. Faith blesses us with perfection and holiness. God can take our little faith, even if it's as weak and little as a mustard seed, and turn it into righteousness in His name.

Second, faith blesses us with grace. Romans 4:16 says, "For this reason it is by faith, in order that it may be in accordance with grace." Do we need some grace? If so, we'd better have some faith. Although grace is an undeserved, unmerited, free gift of God, faith invokes grace. We all need grace. "For by grace are ye saved through faith" (Ephesians 2:8). Faith ignites grace and sets grace on fire. Faith sends grace running to a lost sinner. Faith sends grace running in our time of need, in our adversity, in our trials and tribulations, in our wickedness, in our evilness, in our wrongness. Faith sends grace to us to hug us and love us when we aren't loveable.

Finally, a third thing about faith is that it guarantees the promises of God: " For this reason it is by faith, in order that it may be in accordance with grace, so that the promise will be guaranteed"

(Romans 4:16). Faith undergirds the promises. Faith guarantees the promises of God. I don't know about you, but I'm standing on the promises. Are you standing on the promises? The songwriter said, "I'm standing on the promises of Christ my King, through eternal ages let His praises ring." If you're standing on the promises, you'd better have faith. If you're standing on the promises with no faith, you're standing on shifting, sinking sand. We must have faith. We are indeed blessed through faith.

If we want to be blessed, keep the faith and give God glory. Romans 4:20 says, "He staggered not at the promise of God through unbelief; but was strong in faith, giving glory to God." Abraham was strong in the faith, giving glory to God. Abraham kept the faith and gave glory to God. If we want to be blessed, keep the faith and give glory to God. We are indeed blessed through faith.

Faith is the key that unlocks the door of blessings. Faith lets us please God and be blessed. Faith pleases God and faith blesses us. The promise is that if we please God, He will bless us.

Faith in God undergirds the promises of God. God never asks us just to have faith; rather, God asks that we have faith in Him. Having faith in God underwrites (guarantees) the promises of God.

God promised Abraham, the father of faith, multiple blessings, including the promise that "I will bless your seed." We are all of the seed of Abraham. Therefore, all the blessings that were promised to Abraham are available to us. There is a definite relationship between faith and blessings. Three things concerning faith that relate to blessings are 1) faith blesses us with righteousness, 2) faith blesses us with grace, and 3) faith guarantees the promises of God.

Chapter 11
Being Blessed By God— Also Means Being Blessed Through Affliction

In the 119th Psalm, the psalmist declared, "It is good for me that I was afflicted, that I may learn Your statutes" (verse 71). I want us to briefly look at the two key words in this one verse—and those two key words are good and afflicted. The word "good"—literally means in the Hebrew language—well-pleasing, fruitful, useful and profitable. The word "afflicted"—literally means in the Hebrew language the state of oppression or to be humbled.

How can we be blessed through affliction? This is the question that is on all of our minds. What is so good, useful or fruitful about going through? Where is the blessing in going through or experiencing afflictions in life?

Remember, at the onset of this book, we looked at the Bible to develop a better understanding of the words blessed and bless. As we looked at those two words in light of just what the Bible teaches, the discovery was made that blessings from God are not just exclusively limited to "tangible blessings", but rather they also include "spiritual blessings." And this topic, "Being Blessed Through Affliction", is one of those topics that highlights aspects of the spiritual blessings, and not something that is temporal, physical or earthly.

But......again the question is, "Where is the blessing in going through?" How do we mature to the point of blessing God or praising

God due to our affliction? Or, better yet, how do we see the benefits of God towards us in the midst of our afflictions?

In a nut shell, when I look at this psalm, David teaches us how we are blessed in the midst of our afflictions. When you read this psalm—not just vs. 71, but really beginning with verse 49, David testifies that affliction can bring us closer to God. And, secondly, that affliction can be used to bring glory to God. Affliction, which comes in various ways, can be packaged in many different ways. Affliction can be a sickness that just won't get well. Affliction can be a pain that just won't stop hurting or an addiction that seemingly just can't be overcome. Affliction can be a handicap that is permanent. Affliction can be an illness that may be terminal. Affliction can be nervousness that can't be calmed, a problem that can't be solved, or a mess that can't be cleaned. Affliction comes in many bags, packaged in many ways. But in whichever way it comes.......at the end of the day.......after you have gone though the bouts of affliction......it ought to bring you closer to God, and God should have received the glory.

Trusting God in the Midst of Affliction

Here is our dilemma—we have a problem trusting in God's Word in the time of affliction. We too often focus on the affliction rather than trusting in the Word of God. We've become preoccupied with what we are going through.

A preacher told a story of when he was having some tremendous problems in his church. An elderly woman invited him to her house for lunch. She fixed him a nice meal. He wanted to talk about his problems, but she just wanted to show him a picture of Daniel in the lion's den.

She took him into her family room and showed him a huge picture of Daniel in the lion's den. She asked him what he saw in the picture. He said that he saw lions. She told him to keep looking. All he could see was a man and some lions. The old lady told him to keep on looking, but all he could see were the lions. Then she told him to look at Daniel and tell her what Daniel was doing.

Maybe you've seen this picture. Daniel is not looking at the lions. In the picture, Daniel has his face toward the heavens.

And, when we're in the lion's den, the problem is that we are focusing on the lion. The Word of God says, don't focus on the lion, but, "look to the hills from whence cometh your help" (Psalm 121:1). Focus on God. If there's any affliction in our lives, we must stop focusing on our problems and look at the Word of God. Delight yourself in the Word of God. Remember, God's word declares , "All things work together for the good of those who love the Lord and are the called according to His purpose (Romans 8:28).

The writer of Psalm 119 was going through something, but he didn't focus on the problem. Instead, he focused on the Word of God.

A Lesson From A Psalmist

The emphasis in this psalm is on what is good in the life of the believer. The Hebrew word *tob* is used repeatedly in these verses and can be translated good, pleasant, beneficial, precious, delightful, and right. God does what is good because God is good and because what He does is "according to his word", and His Word is good (v. 39). Neither His character nor His Word will ever change, so, "God is good.......PERIOD."

The psalmist says, "Before I was afflicted, I acted like a complete fool. Before I was afflicted, I went astray, but now I have kept Thy Word." The psalmist says, "I went astray, but now I have kept Thy Word, I'm back in Your will. I went astray, but now I'm keeping Your Word. I'm walking in the way. But as I look back over it, I can truly say it was good for me to have been afflicted that I might learn Your Word. If I hadn't been afflicted, I may not have known Your Word. Your Word is more precious to me now. I went astray and You taught me Your Word. Your Word brought me back. And to me now Your Word is more precious than anything on earth. There is nothing more valuable to me than Your Word." The word of God is better than gold and silver. It gives what gold and silver cannot purchase. It is more refining, and can make you a better person. It is more enriching, and can make you a wealthier man. It is more distinguishing, and can make me a greater woman. It is more sustaining, and can make you a stronger believer. It is more preserving, and can make you a safer man. It is more satisfying, and can make you a happier person. Silver and Gold, silver and Gold.....I would rather have JESUS.....HIS WORD than silver and Gold! The person of faith does not live by the priorities and values of the world but puts the will of God and the word of God ahead of everything else. When we find the good treasures of truth in the precious Word of God, we rejoice in the goodness of the Lord and have no desire to wallow in the things of this world. No matter what our situation may be, we can affirm from our hearts, "God is good all the time!"

God overrules evil and from it brings good. The psalmist had disobeyed the Word of God and gone astray. He had sinned—whether flagrant, purposed and planned or out of ignorance—the point is he sinned. But God in His love sent affliction to discipline him. At the time, this discipline was not pleasant, but it brought God's servant back to the place of obedience, so it was worth it. However, there are times when we are obedient and we still experience suffering, but God uses that suffering to mature us and teach us His word. Charles Spurgeon said that the promises of God shine the brightest in the furnace of affliction. There are times when suffering comes from the enemies of God, whose hearts are insensible, but the Lord can even use godless opposition for our good and His. The most evil act ever performed on this earth was the crucifixion of the Lord of Glory on a cross, yet God used that to bring His salvation to the world.

This psalmist also teaches us that God uses affliction to correct us and humble us. There are some lessons that can only be learned in adversity. There are some lessons that can only be learned in the dark shadows of life. The songwriter said it well when he said if I had not had problems, how would I have ever known that God can solve them? The psalmist said, "Before I was afflicted I went astray." The truth of the matter is that God sometimes has to punish us or chastise us to make us do right. Like any loving parent, God often has to discipline us, punish us and sometimes slap us on the hand. Sometimes He has to take a switch to our legs. And at other times we are so hardheaded, He has to hit us in the head with a two-by-four. All God's punishment and chastisement are done in love, therefore, God could never be locked up for abusing one of His children.

An Opportunity To Bless God

Affliction can be used to bring glory to God. In John 9, Jesus meets a blind man and his parents. The religious folks asked Jesus, "Why is this man blind?" More specifically, they said, "Who sinned? Did his parents sin or did he sin? Why is he blind?" Jesus said, "Neither. He's blind to bring glory, to bring the manifestations of the power of God where everybody can see the good works that God has."

Whatever the affliction in your life might be, we ought to delight in this word -just know that it can bring glory to God. Paul said, "I'm not going to brag about my revelations, but I'm going to brag about my infirmities. I'm going to brag about the thorn in my flesh, my affliction, because it brings glory to God. So the power of Christ can rest on me" (2 Corinthians 12:7-9).

We, like Paul, have a thorn in the flesh. God uses our thorn to keep us from going astray; when we went astray, God put the thorn in our flesh to bring us back to where we should be.

God still uses our thorn to keep us from thinking too much of ourselves. Maybe your body and mind were once afflicted with alcohol addiction that would not go away. An addiction that caused you much pain and much affliction. An addiction that you could not solve by yourself. But, Jesus lifted your affliction and now you can truly say, like the psalmist, it was good that I was afflicted. Before I was afflicted, I had gone astray, but my affliction taught me to trust in God. My affliction brought me on the right track!

Even now, when we begin to think too much of ourselves, God just kind of twists our thorn and lets us know we are headed in the wrong direction!

We can be blessed through our affliction because affliction brings us closer to God, and God can be glorified through our afflictions. The psalmist in the 119 Psalm and the apostle Paul, speaking to the church at Corinth, teaches us powerful lessons about being blessed through affliction. The psalmist proclaims that he had gone astray, but his affliction corrected him. Therefore it was good that he was afflicted. The apostle Paul proclaims that his affliction of "a thorn in the flesh" provided a great opportunity to glorify God. We learn that through affliction we grow closer to God because God comforts us in our afflictions, and we are disciplined and corrected by our afflictions. Through it all, we are blessed through afflictions because our afflictions provide an excellent opportunity for us to bless God.

That is why I like Romans 5:1-5 so much, "Therefore, having been justified by faith, we have peace with God through our Lord Jesus Christ, through whom we also have obtained our introduction by faith into this grace in which we stand; and we exult in hope of the glory of God. AND NOT ONLY THIS, but we also exult in our tribulations, knowing that tribulation brings about perseverance; and perseverance proven character; and proven character, hope; AND HOPE DOES NOT disappoint; because the love of God has been poured out within our hearts through the Holy Spirit who was given to us."

What is the blessing in affliction? Our afflictions will draw us closer to God. Our afflictions will make us stronger men and women of God. Our afflictions will make us wiser. Our afflictions will make us better. Our afflictions will remind us that our hope does not disappoint or let us down. The reason is that our hope is built on nothing less than Jesus, his blood and righteousness. We dare not trust the sweetest frame, but wholly lean on Jesus and His name. On Christ the solid rock we are going to stand. All other ground is sinking sand.

Chapter 12

Being Blessed By God— Also Means Being Blessed Through Perseverance

Recently, I was in a bank not known for its fast service. I was in a hurry and the line was long and I needed to get back to the church. After looking at my watch several times, I decided I would hold on and stand there for a while. But the people in line were restless and began to drop out of line. One man became disgusted, dropped out, and left. The next man dropped out.......and this went on for a while. All together—about five people dropped out of line. The next thing I knew, I was first in line.

And that is when this spiritual truth hit me—we must learn not to get out of line. Believers are dropping out of the blessing line every day—all because we don't have the spirit of perseverance! Many saints are giving up to quickly......giving up to fast........don't have the patience nor the faith to hang in there until God says the warfare is over. We must stay in the line that we may be next on God's blessing agenda. We must stay in the line; hold on and keep on praying. You can only be blessed by God if you persevere. The Apostle Paul put it this way in Galatians 6:9, "Be not weary in well-doing, for in due time you will reap if you faint not."

The word "perseverance" literally means or is defined as a steady persistence in a course of action, or purpose (or state) in spite of difficulties, obstacles or discouragement. So, again I say no matter what is going on, no matter how difficult it may be or how dark it may look , don not get out of line.

A great Biblical illustration or character to look at is the life and times of Jacob.

Jacob was one who held on until his change came. Jacob told God I will not let you go until you bless me. Here is God, and this man is saying, "I won't let you go until you bless me." God said, "What's your name?" He said, "My name is Jacob."

God said, "No, your name used to be Jacob, but your change has come. The name Jacob means deceiver, a sup planter, a trickster. No longer is your name Jacob, but your name is Israel, which means prince that now has power with God because you have prevailed with God and with man." Jacob held on for his blessing. Jacob held on until his change came.

Likewise, we need to hold on until our change comes. We cannot get out of line. We must stay in line and hold fast for there is a light at the end of the tunnel. We must hold fast; there is a blessing on the other side of through. We are blessed through perseverance.

That is how the story ends, but how do we make it to the other side of through? We see how the story ends, that is the picture we ought to paint and hang before us every day from this point on. When you get discouraged, pull out your picture of how it is going to be at the end. But, how do w make it to the other side of through? How do we make it from point A to point B without fainting?

When you look at the story of Jacob—you have to remember that Jacob basically stole two things from his twin brother (Esau). He stole the birthright and the blessing. He stole the birthright, by making a proposition to Esau to sell his birthright to him for the price of a bowl of red beans. The birthright—moved him from the youngest son, to the position of the eldest son—which meant for Jacob a greater inheritance. But, he also stole the blessing by deceiving his dying father (by masquerading as Esau). At the news of Esau being deceived and tricked yet again, Esau decides and makes up his mind to kill his own brother.

In the scripture referenced (Genesis 32), approximately twenty years have passed. Jacob has been living the life of a liar and looking over his shoulder because Esau may be coming over the hill at any minute. Sometimes our change doesn't come until we get tired of running. Jacob was tired of looking over his shoulder. When we get sick and tired of being sick and tired, that is when our change comes.

If we don't get our blessings God's way, our blessings will haunt us. We may think we are blessed right now but if our blessing is not God-approved, our blessing will haunt us. Father Isaac said to Jacob, "I know you tricked me, but I'm still going to bless you." Isaac could have changed his mind when he found out that Jacob had tricked him, but he blessed him anyway. But it does no good for our earthly daddy to bless us if God doesn't bless us. Our mother might leave us the family house, but we need God's blessing on it. Our daddy may leave us the family estate, but we need God's blessing on it. Jacob finally received God's blessings in Genesis 28:10-17. And for 20 years......he was running from Esau, when he had already been blessed by God! You have to remember that even before he was born, God had already prophesied that it would be the younger of the two who would be the vessel to bless all nations.

Jacob's story goes that when he hears that Esau is in the land, a day finally came when Jacob stopped running. He stopped running and started praying. In Jacob praying and seeking the Lord's deliverance. In Jacob's mind, he was facing a desperate and hopeless situation. He had no hope other than to cast himself upon God, and this he did. Only God could help him. Notice his prayer. First, Jacob acknowledged God as the God of his fathers, Abraham and Isaac (Genesis 32:9). By doing this he was addressing God as Elohim, the true God of heaven and earth, the God of all creation and power. But note, he also addressed God as the LORD (Jehovah, Yahweh), who had called him to return to the promised land and to his relatives, and who had promised to be with him (Genesis 32:9). By this he was declaring God to be the LORD of salvation and redemption, the very One who could help and deliver him. Secondly, Jacob then confessed his own unworthiness. He confessed that he was not worthy even of the least of God's mercy and kindness. He was not worthy of God's faithfulness which God had so abundantly showered upon him throughout his life. Jacob was confessing that he had always been unworthy and still was. Also, Jacob acknowledged God's blessing: that God had taken him when he had nothing but a staff in his hand and given him everything he now had, wealth so great that he could divide it into two large groups (Genesis 32:10). Finally, Jacob cried for deliverance from Esau, cried out because he was afraid (Genesis 32:11).

What is our hope when an offended person threatens us or refuses to make peace with us? Jacob shows us. Our hope is prayer, crying out to God for deliverance.

A Wrestling Match

Jacob was left alone and he wrestled with a man until the break of day. He wrestled with him at night. We don't know whether we're reading about a vision or dream or an actuality, but we do know that it was night and many things happen at night. God works at night. Here is the message for you, as dark as it may seem in your life right now.......just know that God does some of His best work at night! This text states that Jacob was prevailing in the wrestling match. Jacob was wrestling with God and for a while it seems as if he was winning.

In my imagination, I believe Jacob had God in a full Nelson. God didn't hit Jacob. God just touched his thigh. It looks like Jacob was winning the battle, and God just touched his thigh. But even with his thigh out of joint, Jacob was still holding on. He knew for sure by now that his arms were too short to box with God. He knew that the only way, the only reason he was prevailing was by the grace of God. He knew that God had just let him win for a while.

Jacob had come to the point where he realized he couldn't win over God, but he still held on. And Jacob told God, "I'm going to hold on. You've knocked my thigh out of joint. There's no telling what you might do to me next. I know I'm not winning this thing, but I'm going to hold on. My thigh is out. I'm hurting. I have pain shooting up in my cranial nerve. My eyes look like they're going to blink out. I feel like I'm going to have a heart attack, but I'm going to hold on. I'm going to hold on until my change comes."

God looked at Jacob and said, "What's your name?" Jacob answered, "My name is Jacob, which means sup-planter. I've been a liar and a trickster all my life." God said, "Your name is no longer Jacob. Your name now is Israel, which means that you have prevailed with God and with man, and I'm going to bless you right here." Jacob named the place Peniel, which means that he had come face to face with God. Jacob left that scene with a limp when the sun came up.

Are we struggling with God? Jacob held on until the sun came out, until the break of day. Break of day may be right around the corner. We must hold on for our blessing. We must hold on through the nighttime. Nighttime may be long. Nighttime may be one big midnight after another. But we must hold on until the sun comes up because scripture declares that "weeping may endure for a night but joy cometh in the morning" (Psalm 30:5).

God is working through the struggles of life. There is a story I love so much about this man who was confined to a hospital room for a rather long stay, while recuperating from a major surgery. At some point during his stay, he noticed that a cocoon had fallen from the limb of a tree that was by his window and fell on the window sill. A few hours after the cocoon had fallen, he noticed that the caterpillar had completed its transformation into a butterfly and was now preparing for its exit from the cocoon into the world. For the remainder of that day, his focus was on that small opening and the struggle of the emergence. He went to sleep, and the next morning he realized that the struggle was still going on. So the man reasoned within himself that something was wrong. He thought that the butterfly had gotten trapped or stuck in the cocoon because the opening was too small. So, the man made a decision to help by taking a pair of scissors and widening the opening so the butterfly wouldn't struggle so much. The man made opening wider and then returned back to his hospital bed. The butterfly did emerge within the next hour. The man was happy. He saw it crawl on the window sill. But that's all it ever did. The man kept waiting for the wings of the butterfly to dry, and then he thought, "It will fly once it dries out." The butterfly dried out, but all it did was crawl on that window sill. That is when it finally dawned on him, that God knows what He is doing. The man realized that God uses the struggle of the butterfly emerging from a small opening in the cocoon to push the necessary juices back into the wings of the butterfly to make it capable for it to fly.

Detachment

Why aren't we blessed? The answer is, "Because of detachment." We have a problem with not being attached. We're not holding on because we have cut ourselves off from the blessing. We have cut ourselves off from the blessing giver. If you abide in God. If you'll hold on to God and His Word holds on to you, you can ask what you will and it shall be done unto you (John 15:7).

We think we are attached when we really are not. Some are deceived by a holy self-righteousness and think they are attached, but they are really off the vine. If we want to be blessed, we have to be on the vine. "I am the true vine, and my Father is the husbandman" (John 15:1). If we're not on the vine, we need to get back on the vine. We must hold on till our blessings come. Winds may blow, but we must stay on the vine. Storms may rise, but we must stay on the vine. Heavy rain may beat down on the vine, but we must stay on the vine until our blessing comes. We must stay on the vine until our change comes.

Being Blessed Requires A Struggle

Not only do we have to persevere, but we have to struggle. In life, anything worth having is worth working for. We shouldn't appreciate anything given to us on a silver platter. That's why God wants us to struggle. If we don't struggle, we will not have any gratitude. If we don't struggle, we will have no thanksgiving. If we have no thanksgiving, we will have no praise. Do we ever wonder why the new generation seems not to have very much gratitude? It's our fault, not theirs. We give them too much. We need to make sure our children work for what they have.

Jacob had to prevail with God and with man. Some of us are very satisfied in our struggle in our relationship with God, but we don't want to struggle in our relationship with other people. Some of us will tithe to God, but disobey God's Word concerning our relationships with other people.

We will disobey Matthew 18:15 that says if we have ought with our brother, we need to go to our brother and confront the fault. We will disobey Matthew 5:23 that says if we bring our gift to the altar and we have ought with our brother, we should leave our gift there and go back and make the situation straight. We disobey these scriptures, which means we are unattached, we are detached. We are not as blessed as God desires because we are not struggling to stay attached to the vine.

Blessings Require Change

We have to persevere in the struggle, and we have to persevere for the change. Jacob persevered till his change came. Jacob's name was changed from Jacob to Israel. The twelve sons of Jacob became the twelve tribes of Israel. Jacob's name, which originally meant trickster, now means prince that has power, that has prevailed with man and with God. If we want to be blessed, some transformation has to take place in our lives. "And be not conformed to this world: but be ye transformed by the renewing of your mind, that ye may prove what is that good, and acceptable, and perfect, will of God" (Romans 12:2). We must experience some transformation.

Hold On in Your Brokenness

If we want to be blessed, we have to be broken. After Jacob had struggled with God, the sun rose and he went away limping because his hip was out of joint. We need to understand that Jacob limped for the rest of his life. His limp represented his brokenness. His limp represented the fact that his deceitful, deceiving, evil spirit was broken. His limp represented that his lying spirit had been broken. Jacob's limp always reminded him of his old self. Any time Jacob's humanity began to rise too much, God would shoot a little pain down in his limp to remind him that his arms were too short to box with God. Jacob was reminded through his limp to stay humble.

Like Jacob, I too have a limp in my life. I am blessed, but I, also like Paul, have a thorn in my flesh. Every time my ego gets inflated, God deflates it with my thorn because He wants to use me and bless me. My limp reminds me of the day that my change came. My limp will remind me that there is a blessing on the other side of through. My limp reminds me that I struggled with Him till I was blessed. My limp will remind me that I always may be next in line. My limp reminds me that we all can be blessed through perseverance, so we should hold on until our blessing comes.

Perseverance is a key factor in being blessed. The familiar scripture narrative that tells of how Jacob wrestled with God and held on until his blessing came teaches us a valuable lesson on perseverance. We learn: 1) if our blessings are not approved by God, they will later haunt us, 2) we must stay attached to the blessing source, 3) to be blessed we must struggle, 4) to be blessed we must change, and 5) to be blessed we must be broken. We ought, therefore, to remain in the line until our change comes because God blesses through our perseverance.

www.ingramcontent.com/pod-product-compliance
Lightning Source LLC
Chambersburg PA
CBHW032006040426
42448CB00006B/500